THE WIZARD of OZ

COLLECTOR'S TREASURY

Jay Scarfone   William Stillman

Photographs by Tim McGowan

Schiffer Publishing Ltd

1469 Morstein Road, West Chester, Pennsylvania 19380

Published by Schiffer Publishing, Ltd.
1469 Morstein Road
West Chester, Pennsylvania 19380
Please write for a free catalog.
This book may be purchased from the publisher.
Please include $2.95 postage.
Try your bookstore first.

Printed in the United States of America.
ISBN: 0-88740-430-8

We are interested in hearing from authors with book ideas on related
topics.

DEDICATION

For Fred, Royal Secretary of Oz—For his friend-
ship, unconditional support and belief in this
project, and for his generous loan of so many
wonderful pieces of "Oz and ends," we dedicate
this book.

Acknowledgments

The authors wish to extend a heart-felt thanks to those individuals who were gracious enough to give of their time, energy, and enthusiasm in assisting to make this book a reality: Jane Albright, The Alexander Mitchell Library (David Rave), Bill Beem, Tom and Eileen Bonawitz, Camden House Auctioneers (Michael Schwartz and Tawny Thornton), Cinema Arts (David Graveen), Audrea Cohen, Myles Cohen, Douglas Congdon-Martin, Crystallite (Marlon Woolf), Dave Grossman Creations (Flora Spuhl), Bill Day, Cathi Dentler, Cynthia Dorfman, Rita Dubas, Deya Durkatz, Sam Ervais, The Franklin Mint (Robin Lynch), Blair Frodelius, Philip Gamble, Michael Gessel, Goebel Miniatures (Travis Tokuyama). JoAnn Groves, Ted Hake, Michael Patrick Hearn, Susan Heath, Russ King, Barbara S. Koelle, Norm Lazarson, Tod Machin, Rob Roy MacVeigh, Tim McGowan, Marge Meisinger, Fred M. Meyer, David Moyer, Maureen Nalevanko, Cordelia and Thomas Platt, Meinhardt Raabe, N. Thomas Rogness, Chris Russell and the Halloween Queen, Dana Ryan, Tom Sando, Dede Schaeffer, Peter Schiffer and the Schiffer team, Larry Schlick, Jean Schreiner, Patricia E. Smith, Laura and Rickey Spann, Chris Sterling, Tricia Trozzi, Turner Entertainment (Polly Savell, Kip Frey, Lois Sloane and Carol Postal), Elaine Willingham, World Doll (Arline Alfieri), Peggy Yale.

The decorative illustrations printed throughout this book were reproduced from the first edition of *The Wonderful Wizard of Oz* (1900, George M. Hill Company).

Unless credited otherwise, all collectibles and memorabilia illustrated are from the authors' collections as photographed by Tim McGowan Studios, Lebanon, Pennsylvania.

Contents

Introduction

As far back as we can remember, both of us have been fascinated and enchanted by the story of *The Wizard of Oz*. Like so many others, our own interest in the Land of Oz began with a childhood attachment to the classic Metro-Goldwyn-Mayer film version of the story through its traditional television broadcasts each year. As adults, we would come to discover that our admiration for Oz had not only sustained itself over time, but had in fact grown into an obsessive enthusiasm that compelled us to learn as much as we could about every aspect of Ozian history and collect artifacts pertaining to its mythic culture.

As the year 1989 marked the momentous golden anniversary of the release of the MGM motion picture, we were afforded the perfect opportunity to "go public" with our affection toward the story and its characters by co-authoring *The Wizard of Oz: The Official Fiftieth Anniversary Pictorial History* (1989, Warner Books). This book, for those who are unfamiliar with it, was intended to visually document the legacy of the film itself in addition to the legend of Oz in general. In so doing, part of our overall strategy included illustrating numerous (yet relatively limited) examples of Oz collectibles and memorabilia from the past nine decades. To

our delight, readers responded with over-whelming excitement for this aspect of the book and those who were themselves Oz collectors indicated they were actually using *The Pictorial History* as a reference tool. Flattering as this may have been, the truth of the matter was that this particular volume had not been designed to serve as a true "collector's guide" and therefore left many questions unanswered in addition to raising new ones. That being the case, we soon found ourselves deluged with inquiries from Oz collectors and dealers alike regarding much of the memorabilia pictured in the book, not to mention various other items that weren't illustrated. Of the many responses received, typical comments and questions included the following:

"Your book has inspired me to start collecting *Wizard of Oz* memorabilia. Can you tell me how to get started?"
"How and where can I find Oz collectibles?"
"I have a few things in my collection that weren't in your book. Can you identify them for me?"
"What is Oz memorabilia worth?" and—
"I never knew there was so much Oz memorabilia!"

Part of the reason many Oz collectibles are so elusive (particularly the early, vintage material) is that, until recent years, the vast majority of mass-marketed Ozzy merchandise was geared toward young people. Consequently, in the boundless enthusiasm of youth, books were colored in, dolls were broken, and toys and games were fervently played with, worn out, and—ultimately—thrown away. Then of course there are those materials such as advertising posters, store displays, and magazine and newspaper publicity that were produced for intended short-term use. Constructed in their customary non-durable fashion, these items were typically discarded in most cases upon fulfillment of their designated purposes. What's more, even when surviving *Wizard of Oz* memorabilia does surface, one often faces a dilemma with respect to identification. This is because (regrettably) so much of what has been issued over the years is undated or devoid of any markings that might provide a clue as to manufacturer or era produced. Thus, an individual is frequently left with only an educated guess, oftentimes based purely on the "look" of a given item.

As we began to do our best to acknowledge the inflow of inquiries from those who were enthusiastic enough to share their thoughts with us, we soon realized that what our fellow aficionados were experiencing was not surprising. Although there have been a few scattered references regarding Oz memorabilia in books and magazine articles, never before had an attempt been made to document at length the toys, dolls, posters, games, and other ephemera directly inspired by the Land of Oz and its citizens. With this in mind, our response was to compile *The Wizard of Oz Collector's Treasury*.

Our primary goal in assembling *The Wizard of Oz Collector's Treasury* was to furnish readers with an insightful, full-color visual reference guide to almost a century of Ozzy merchandise, memorabilia, and collectibles. In so doing, we felt the most functional way to present the book would be to categorize all items as specifically as possible so as to allow users to—hopefully—locate an item in question with relative ease. Though we realize that the value guide section of this book is bound to be controversial, there seems to be a need among both collectors and dealers for a means of effectively estimating and recognizing fair market values. In the interest of Oz enthusiasts, it is our genuine hope that this volume will help to answer some of the questions that have plagued us all for years—as well as those that surely lie ahead on that yellow brick road to our future collecting adventures. (Practicality aside, we would be satisfied in simply knowing that this photographic ensemble provided just plain fun and enjoyment for dedicated Ozophiles everywhere!)

While we'd like to consider *The Wizard of Oz Collector's Treasury* as being fairly comprehensive, it is certainly not exhaustive in its research. This is partly due to the need to be selective and partly because no one truly knows exactly what has been produced in over ninety years' time! Perhaps the most significant omission from this work is an *in-depth* examination of the various editions of the Oz books themselves. This was, however, a conscious choice of ours since such a feat has already merited the attention of expert Oz book historians and its own complete volume entitled *Bibliographia Oziana* (1976, revised 1988; The International Wizard of Oz Club, Inc.). Instead, we have pictured many of the *Wizard of Oz* and Oz book abridgements and adaptations that have appeared over the years. We likewise have chosen to avoid attempting to document movie costumes and props or original works of art as these items were not mass-produced and may be considered one of a kind.

Still, we'd like to think that, together with those who share our genuine love of Oz and who were so generous in contributing their own knowledge and artifacts, we've made a collaborative effort in creating a colorful tribute to several generations of "Oz and ends," testament to the enduring popularity of the wonderful *Wizard of Oz.*

Enjoy!

Jay Scarfone
William Stillman

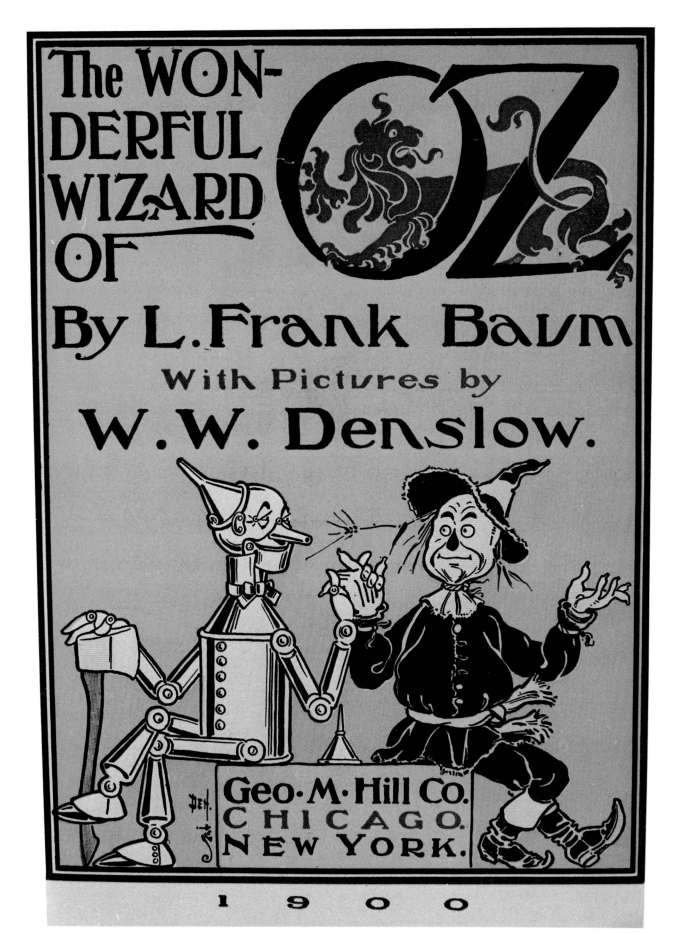

The WONDERFUL WIZARD OF OZ

By L. Frank Baum

With Pictures by W.W. Denslow.

Geo. M. Hill Co.
CHICAGO.
NEW YORK.

1900

The History of

Collectibles

For those of us who cherish the delightful and lovably eccentric inhabitants of the Land of Oz, the desire to obtain and collect tangible reminders of our faithful allegiance seems a natural extension of our affectionate interest. After all, who among us as children (or even adults!) have not envisioned ourselves with Dorothy and her companions in that most magical of places? Accumulating Ozzy artifacts—be it books, toys, promotional materials or other ephemera—appreciating the vivid colors, charming characters and childhood memories such items evoke, enables us to place ourselves one step closer to making such escapist fantasies realities, however temporary those occasions may be.

It has been over nine decades since author L. Frank Baum (1856-1919) and illustrator W.W. Denslow (1856-1915) collaborated on what has since been deemed the first truly American fairy tale, *The Wonderful Wizard of Oz* (1900, George M. Hill Co.). Baum's gifted ability to make the most fantastic of circumstances perfectly plausible, his capacity to imbue outlandish creatures with warmth and humanity and his fondness for puns combined with Denslow's brilliant color plates, line drawings and decorative illustrations produced a lavish volume which, for the time, was innovative both in style and presentation. The story of how Baum (and subsequent "Royal Historians of Oz") came to

The cover binding and title page of the first edition of *The Wonderful Wizard of Oz* by L. Frank Baum, illustrated by W.W. Denslow and published by George M. Hill Company in 1900. The book's title page art would be modified for an advertising poster which billed the story as "the funniest child's book ever published." *Courtesy Cathi Dentler.*

A 1900 book poster promoted the newly published *Wonderful Wizard of Oz* in addition to Baum and Denslow's first collaborative efforts, *Father Goose: His Book* (1899) and *The Songs of Father Goose* (1900). *Courtesy Michael Patrick Hearn.*

write an entire series of Oz and other children's books has been well documented by numerous scholars and authorities throughout the years in much greater depth than the overview to follow (refer to the Bibliography on page 256). Therefore, rather than reiterate the most specific details of that rich heritage (which have since passed into legend), we merely wish to provide readers with a brief examination of Ozian historical events which led to the evolution of over ninety years' worth of merchandise, memorabilia, and collectibles.*

THE MAGIC BEGINS

During the early part of the century, book- and comic-character-inspired merchandise was not unheard of, being chiefly patterned after traditional fairy tales or favorite contemporary creations. Cinderella, Little Red Riding Hood,

Lewis Carroll's Alice, and Palmer Cox's mischievous Brownies (popular since their 1883 "discovery") found their way onto the marketplace in the form of figurines, games, dolls and premiums. Likewise, R.F. Outcault's Yellow Kid and Buster Brown received equal marketing exploitation at this time, as would a parade of renowned characters to follow including Foxy Grandpa, the Katzenjammer Kids, Happy Hooligan, Maggie and Jiggs, Rose O'Neill's Kewpies, and, the king of all comic personalities, Mickey Mouse.

In retrospect then, it may seem surprising to those unfamiliar with the earliest roots of Ozian beginnings that, given the popularity of the Oz book series, more merchandise wasn't marketed outside of the sparse publicity and advertising gimmicks most often generated by publishers. Aside from book posters advertising the 1900 publication of *The Wonderful Wizard of Oz* (a tradition that would continue in touting the entire Oz book series), there were no further promotional materials issued that year by George M. Hill Company, the book's publisher, despite nearly unanimous public and critical acceptance of the story.

Though his publishers may have lacked adequate resources and backing, author L. Frank Baum had recognized the novelty of his Oz characters from the outset. As one of the motivational aspirations throughout his later adult

*Authors' note: Aside from the various product advertisements, the memorabilia illustrated in this section of the book is considered especially uncommon and is not reflected in the Value Guide. It is presented here solely for the reader's enjoyment.

life, Baum consistently sought to count himself among those elite colleagues who could readily point with pride to their own book or comic characters, the ensuing merchandise spawned by their popularity *and* all the inherent financial trappings. To a point, Baum attained his goal, but ofttimes his visionary ventures fell short of mass acceptance beyond his literary Land of Oz. Perhaps as consolation of sorts, the comparatively limited use of Oz character promotion and endorsement over the years did inadvertently provide young readers with the opportunity to rely upon a valuable childhood resource: imagination.

One of Baum's earliest auxiliary endeavors as an author came shortly after publication of *The Wonderful Wizard of Oz*. He and Chicago composer Paul Tietjens began to rough out the narrative for stage production as an extravagantly mounted comic opera, with W.W. Denslow serving as costume designer. Despite many character and plot changes, script revisions and a professional falling-out with Denslow, Baum's dream of seeing *The Wizard of Oz* brought to life was realized on June 16, 1902 at Chicago's Grand Opera House to largely glowing critical approval. In addition to several unique special effects and breathtaking scenery—most notably the poppy field scene—the chief focus of the

The Russell Morgan Company printed many magnificently lithographed posters for *The Wizard of Oz* stage play. The 1902 print shown here pictured the warm camaraderie of vaudeville team Fred Stone, as the Scarecrow, and Dave Montgomery, as the Tin Woodman. *From a reproduction courtesy Michael Gessel.*

The Opulence of Oz: One of the Strobridge Litho Company's 1904 *Wizard of Oz* posters illustrated the play's celebrated poppy field scene which featured over two dozen chorus girls disguised as poisonous blossoms. Singled out by critics as the most inspired of the show's tableaux, one scribe remarked "...it deserves to rank among the very best achievements in modern scenic art." A first-time viewing of the spectacle prompted an emotional response from author L. Frank Baum who commented that "...a wave of gratitude swept over me that I had lived to see the sight." The slumbering travelers included the supplementary characters Pastoria II, Tryxie Tryfle and Dorothy's pet calf!, Imogene. The group was rescued from their predicament by Locasta, the Good Witch of the North, who quelled the flowers' deadly scent with an icy snowstorm—a device later incorporated into the script of the 1939 MGM film. *From a reproduction courtesy Barbara S. Koelle.*

Two Russell Morgan posters circa 1902-04 of the Tin Man and Scarecrow from *The Wizard of Oz* musical production. David Montgomery's skull cap and stark white makeup was strongly reminiscent of G.L. Fox's "Humpty Dumpty" character. The fairy tale play of the same title was one of the longest running theatrical productions of the late 1800s. *From reproductions courtesy Michael Gessel.*

spectacle of the production in lavishly lithographed color while souvenir programs and penny postcards of Montgomery and Stone in play scenes were available for sale in theater lobbies. On April 15, 1903, the Majestic Theater commemorated the one hundredth performance by issuing small metal jewelry boxes—embossed, dated, and ornamented with a three-dimensional Cowardly Lion—to patrons of its Wednesday matinee. Similarly, small collapsible metal cups were given as souvenirs to those in attendance for the two hundredth performance on July 11, 1903, and little cardboard figures of the Scarecrow and Tin Man were reportedly distributed to children in the audience on several occasions as well. On a widespread scale, sheet music of the show's songs (including complete song folios) was sold beginning in 1902, largely through M. Witmark & Sons, and at least two of the musical numbers were printed as newspaper supplements as part of the press coverage the play received. Meanwhile, two pirated publications appeared at this time; the first being *A Tin Man's Joke Book*, the other being a pamphlet incorporating the *Wonderful Wizard of Oz* color book plates—both unauthorized by either Baum or Denslow.

For the 1904 return engagements of *The Wizard of Oz*, the Strobridge Litho Company printed a series of beautifully rendered posters of noteworthy scenes from the famed production. This poster depicted a special effects sequence wherein Scarecrow (Fred Stone) was effectively shadow-boxed and appeared to be dismembered, only to be reassembled by a perplexed Dorothy (Anna Laughlin) and the Tin Man (Dave Montgomery), dressed as a streetcar driver! *From a reproduction courtesy Barbara S. Koelle.*

play was the comic antics of David C. Montgomery as the Tin Woodman and Fred A. Stone as an amazingly limber Scarecrow. The popularity of their *Wizard* performances solidified their appeal as a vaudeville team and, in later runs of the play, entire songs and routines were added to take advantage of their comedic celebrity. After fourteen weeks in Chicago, the play company moved to New York's Majestic Theater on January 20, 1903, running for 293 performances and establishing itself as one of Broadway history's greatest successes at that time. The show made a return engagement to New York in 1904 for several weeks before continuing in road show productions into the next decade.

The original theatrical advertising posters for the play conveyed the excitement, humor, and

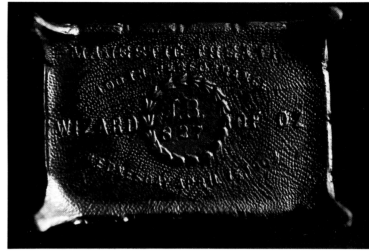

Two views of the metal souvenir jewelry box issued to matinee attenders by New York's Majestic Theater to commemorate the "100th performance-WIZARD OF OZ-Wednesday, April 15, 1903," as was inscribed on the container's bottom. *Courtesy Michael Patrick Hearn, photos: David Moyer.*

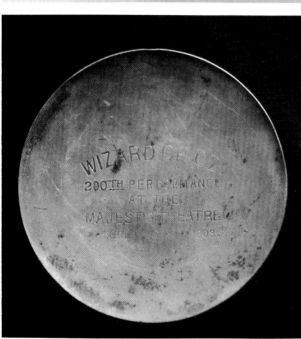

Following the success of *The Wonderful Wizard of Oz*, Baum responded with a sequel ultimately published as *The Marvelous Land of Oz* (1904, Reilly & Britton). Detailing the "further adventures of the Scarecrow and Tin Woodman," the book was accompanied by a dedication to Montgomery and Stone and endpapers incorporating photographs of their *Wizard* personae. It was further embellished with carefully rendered watercolor and pen-and-ink drawings by accomplished draftsman John R. Neill (1877-1943), whose illustrations for this and the next thirty-four Oz books would become as much an indelible and inseparable component of Oz iconography as Denslow's *Wonderful Wizard of Oz* drawings.

To mark the two hundredth performance of *The Wizard of Oz* on Saturday, July 11, 1903, the Majestic Theater dispensed collapsible metal cups which, like the previously distributed jewelry boxes, were embossed to honor the occasion. *Courtesy Michael Patrick Hearn; photos: David Moyer.*

Two of six color lithographed wallpaper panels designed by W.W. Denslow measured 30 inches long and pictured the characters popularized in *The Wizard of Oz* stage production for which the artist also created the costumes. *Courtesy The Baum Bugle.*

13

During the summer of 1904, the first issue of the *Ozmapolitan* rolled off the presses and into the eager hands of children long awaiting L. Frank Baum's sequel to *The Wonderful Wizard of Oz*. Publishers Reilly & Britton issued the small four-page "newspaper" to publicize *The Marvelous Land of Oz*. *Courtesy* The Baum Bugle.

As part of an agreement to aggressively promote the new Oz book, publishers Reilly & Britton took out full-page magazine and newspaper ads and distributed the *Ozmapolitan* newspaper to keep readers updated on "current events" in Oz. They likewise published a song written by Baum and play collaborator Paul Tietjens entitled "What Did the Woggle-Bug Say?" as inspired by the oversized insect character featured in *The Marvelous Land of Oz* (a character that the author would briefly seek to exploit in the manner of numerous comic personalities effectively merchandised by their creators at that time).

Abetting the extensive promotion for his works, Baum busily wrote the text of a Sunday comic page illustrated by cartoonist Walt McDougall in the rambling "slapstick" style the author would have preferred for his Oz books. Known to readers as "Queer Visitors From the Marvelous Land of Oz," the weekly feature documented the misadventures had by many of the *Land of Oz*

characters while in the United States. Its publication run began on August 28, 1904 and continued through February 26, 1905. Many newspapers that carried the comic page participated in the "What Did the Woggle-Bug Say?" contest in connection with the feature, a campaign that included disbursement of celluloid "Woggle-Bug" buttons, advertising posters, character postcards, and Parker Brothers' *Wogglebug Game of Conundrums*.

Despite his bitter differences with Baum, W.W. Denslow also pursued his vested interest in the *Wizard* characters as co-copyright holder. Taking advantage of the stage production's popular acclaim, he wrote and pictured *Denslow's Scarecrow and The Tin-Man* (G.W. Dillingham Co.) in 1904. (It told of the two famous characters running away from the Majestic Theater!) Like the Oz books, this full-color booklet and a series of others like it (also bound collectively as *Denslow's Scarecrow and The Tin-Man and Other Stories*) were announced by a book poster on which the illustrator's original Scarecrow was prominent. Between December 10, 1904 and February 18, 1905, a rival comic page to Baum's "Queer Visitors" appeared as "Denslow's Scarecrow and Tin Man." Similar to Baum's strip, the narrative followed the travels of the Scarecrow, Tin Woodman, and Cowardly Lion throughout the United States and South America.

Pursuing his belief in the marketability of his intellectual insectoid character, Baum next penned *The Woggle-Bug Book* (1905, Reilly & Britton) which, like "Queer Visitors," was humorously illustrated by Ike Morgan. Hoping to translate these many intervening efforts and capitalize on the *Wizard*'s success, the author adapted elements from this book and *The Marvelous Land of Oz* for another musical comedy titled *The Woggle-Bug*. Opening at Chicago's Garrick Theater on June 18, 1905, the production was perceived as a weak imitation of *The Wizard of Oz* ("a shabby and dull repetition" of the earlier play, according to one critic!) and closed shortly thereafter on July 12, 1905. The play's score, however, was made available by M. Witmark & Sons in sheet music format.

By public demand, Baum immersed himself further in his Oz creations—a stable and financially secure niche—and in the years that followed wrote *Ozma of Oz* (1907) and *Dorothy and the Wizard in Oz* (1908). He then involved himself in a unique and original publicity venture

The front cover of Reilly & Britton's 1907 advertising brochure announced the publication of Baum's new book (telling "more adventures of little Dorothy in Ozland") entitled *Ozma of Oz*. *Courtesy* The Baum Bugle.

The Patchwork Girl of Oz

To publicize the first new Oz book since 1910, Reilly & Britton distributed full-color illustrations of *The Patchwork Girl of Oz* accompanied on the reverse by an enthusiastic write-up heralding the 1913 return to Oz. *Courtesy the Baum Collection, Alexander Mitchell Library.*

designed to increase Oz awareness through a series of hand-tinted slide and moving picture "lectures" called *Fairylogue and Radio-Plays*, which incorporated bits of the Oz canon to date. Though the author was thoroughly enrapturing as orator, his "travelogues" proved financially draining and he was forced to abandon the project in the end. Selig Polyscope, manufacturers of the *Radio-Plays* film, nonetheless optioned the use of Baum's movies for release as four one-reel silent films in 1910, *The Wonderful Wizard of Oz* being among them.

Ardent young readers insisted Baum continue the Oz stories with *The Road to Oz* (1909) and *The Emerald City of Oz* (1910). Although the author attempted to end the series with the latter title in order to pursue other writings, his youthful public would hear none of it and in 1913 *The Patchwork Girl of Oz* was published. Heralding this return to Oz, Reilly & Britton issued paper Patchwork Girl figures, a cardboard rocking "Woozy" dog and a set of six "Oz books in miniature" written by Baum with accompanying illustrations by John R. Neill. Forerunners of today's Little Golden Books, the small volumes were collectively known as The Little Wizard Series, titles of which included *The Cowardly Lion and the Hungry Tiger*, *Little Dorothy and Toto*, *Tiktok and the Nome King*, *Ozma and the Little Wizard*, *Jack Pumpkinhead and the Sawhorse* and *The Scarecrow and the Tin*

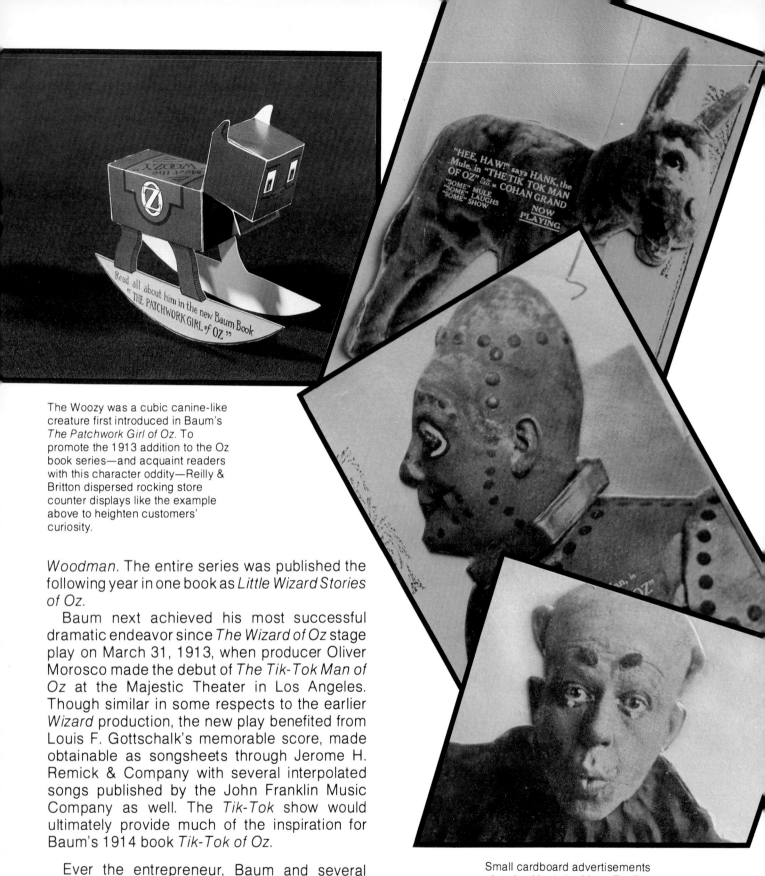

The Woozy was a cubic canine-like creature first introduced in Baum's *The Patchwork Girl of Oz*. To promote the 1913 addition to the Oz book series—and acquaint readers with this character oddity—Reilly & Britton dispersed rocking store counter displays like the example above to heighten customers' curiosity.

Woodman. The entire series was published the following year in one book as *Little Wizard Stories of Oz*.

Baum next achieved his most successful dramatic endeavor since *The Wizard of Oz* stage play on March 31, 1913, when producer Oliver Morosco made the debut of *The Tik-Tok Man of Oz* at the Majestic Theater in Los Angeles. Though similar in some respects to the earlier *Wizard* production, the new play benefited from Louis F. Gottschalk's memorable score, made obtainable as songsheets through Jerome H. Remick & Company with several interpolated songs published by the John Franklin Music Company as well. The *Tik-Tok* show would ultimately provide much of the inspiration for Baum's 1914 book *Tik-Tok of Oz*.

Ever the entrepreneur, Baum and several colleagues also founded the Oz Film Manufacturing Company in Hollywood in 1914. At a time when the motion picture industry was in its infancy, the company began producing five-reel silent pictures of the author's famous stories,

Small cardboard advertisements picturing Hank the Mule, Tik-Tok and the Shaggy Man announced the summer, 1913 Chicago engagement of *The Tik-Tok Man of Oz* at the George M. Cohan Theater. *Courtesy the late Dick Martin.*

Two advertising brochures from October and December 1914 were designed to incite interest in the Oz Film Manufacturing Company's fantasy photoplays. Both pamphlets listed an array of materials obtainable from the company "advertising bureau". These included posters, heralds, advance announcement slides and hand-tinted sets of sixteen stills. *From reproductions courtesy Michael Gessel.*

officially releasing *The Patchwork Girl of Oz* through Paramount's distribution on September 28, 1914. Standard film campaign materials such as posters, stills and press releases were issued in conjunction with the feature at this time and a promotional wooden Woozy was also manufactured. Though it employed special effects, actors affiliated with previous Oz productions, and generous publicity in film periodicals of the day, *The Patchwork Girl* was considered disappointing and childish by adult audiences at large, despite a warm critical reception.

Undaunted, the company continued filming on its luxuriously equipped seven acre lot, producing five features and a few short subjects before folding in 1915. Of the other movies completed, two were Oz features entitled *The Magic Cloak of Oz* and *His Majesty, The Scarecrow of Oz* (later retitled *The New Wizard of Oz*). The latter was composed of story line that would form the basis of Baum's 1915 book *The Scarecrow of Oz*. This new addition to the Oz series was heavily publicized through posters, celluloid advertising buttons, cutout figures and John R. Neill's full-color, sixteen-page *The Oz Toy Book*.

The beginning of each of the Hollywood-based Oz Film Manufacturing Company's silent features opened with actress Vivian Reed's beaming impersonation of Ozma of Oz as inspired by one of John R. Neill's pen-and-ink portraits of the girl ruler. (Note the dark cloth covering Reed's neck and shoulders, giving the illusion that her head is floating mid-air!) *Courtesy the Baum Collection, Alexander Mitchell Library.*

The campaign to publicize Baum's 1915 book, *The Scarecrow of Oz*, included colorful cardboard figures of the beloved title character himself. *Courtesy the late Dick Martin.*

Wizard

Wiggle bug

Toto

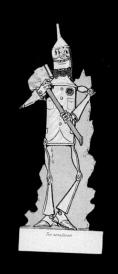

Tin woodman

Glinda

The OZ TOY BOOK

Cut-outs for the Kiddies

JNO. R. NEILL

Dorothy

Patchwork girl

Cowardly Lion

Scarecrow

In later years, Baum grew cautious and less willing to invest in risky business ventures even though he remained faithful in spirit. As such, he found contentment in further writings that included *Rinkitink in Oz* (1916), *The Lost Princess of Oz* (1917) and *The Tin Woodman of Oz* (1918). Before succumbing to a life-long battle with a weak heart complicated by other health problems, the author also completed manuscripts for two more Oz books which were published posthumously as *The Magic of Oz* (1919) and *Glinda of Oz* (1920) by the newly regrouped Reilly & Lee. Upon his deathbed, L. Frank Baum whispered that he would now be able to transcend the Deadly Desert that bordered his mythic country. Shortly afterward, appropriately enough, Reilly & Lee distributed to Baum's young devotees small color maps of the Land of Oz.

THE ROAD TO OZ CONTINUES

Rather than allow the lucrative Oz book series to languish and expire with the passing of L. Frank Baum, Reilly & Lee found a qualified authoress in Philadelphian, Ruth Plumly Thompson (1891-1976), to assume the title "Royal Historian of Oz." No stranger to Oz, Thompson had grown up loving Baum's stories and was keenly aware of the legacy appointed her. Recently established as a writer of fanciful short stories for children, the young journalist began her tenure with 1921's *The Royal Book of Oz*. To ease transition, though, the book was

credited to Baum and merely "enlarged and edited" by Thompson. That same year, Parker Brothers introduced its *The Wonderful Game of Oz*, an elaborate affair issued in homage of the Oz books. It was replete with figural markers depicting Dorothy and her three companions, dice that spelled out "W-I-Z-A-R-D" and a superbly lithographed box cover and game board.

In 1922, Ruth Plumly Thompson's second Oz book was announced via an elaborate bookstore counter display card which pictured the new story's pachyderm protagonist as well as a number of well-known Ozian citizens. *Courtesy* The Baum Bugle.

Opposite page:
Over four dozen popular Oz book characters were printed in full-color for John R. Neill's *The Oz Toy Book*. The sixteen-page booklet was first advertised in Reilly & Britton's July, 1915 catalogue without L. Frank Baum's knowledge or consent—a situation that caused conflict and tension between the author and his publishers. Not only was Baum dissatisfied with the artwork, but memories of W.W. Denslow's independent use of his Oz creations quickly resurfaced. As a consolation, the publishers did not reprint the booklet. Several of the best known characters are shown here along with the booklet's cover, as reprinted by The International Wizard of Oz Club. (Original copies were bound by string.) *Cutouts from private collection.*

Thompson next continued the Oz canon with *Kabumpo in Oz* (1922), heralded by a large cutout poster depicting the story's elephantine hero, *The Cowardly Lion of Oz* (1923), and *Grampa in Oz* (1924). Reilly & Lee issued a clever advertising novelty for the series at this time called "The Scarecrow of Oz Answers Questions by Radio." This curiosity was manufactured by the J.B. Carroll Company of Chicago and consisted of a simple cardboard leaflet with an interior magnetic dial that, once set and folded, would "magically" answer questions about the Oz books. Book sellers made the leaflet available free with the purchase of any Oz title.

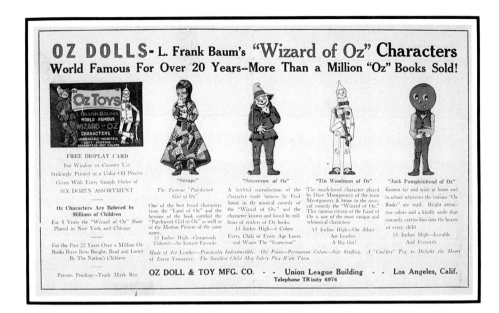

A circa 1924 advertising leaflet listed Frank J. Baum's "Oz Dolls" as inspired by characters popularized by his father, author L. Frank Baum. To authenticate the dolls, it was stated that each stuffed figure would bear the famous writer's "signature," however known examples do not have such a marking. In addition to illustrating the four Oz personalities available, the brochure also pictured the "free display card...given with every sample order of six dozen assortment." *Private collection.*

The year 1925 saw the publication of *The Lost King of Oz* and further publicity for the Oz book series. Having cultivated an interest in his father's characters, Frank J. Baum, (the eldest of L. Frank Baum's four sons) began to market a line of colorful oil-cloth stuffed dolls through his Oz Doll & Toy Manufacturing Company. These included "Scraps" (The Patchwork Girl), "Scarecrow of Oz," "Tin Woodman of Oz" and "Jack Pumpkinhead of Oz." When this proved an unsuccessful venture for young Baum, Reilly & Lee agreed to distribute the Oz Doll Company's remaining stock by cleverly packaging each of the dolls individually with a copy of the Oz book featuring that particular character. The publisher also circulated copies of a play written by Ruth Plumly Thompson entitled "A Day in Oz" and including songs she had co-written the previous year. With Reilly & Lee supplying costumes, props and scenery, the musical was performed in book and department stores across the country, with Thompson herself portraying Dorothy in one Washington, D.C. presentation.

Chadwick Pictures released its silent film version of *The Wizard of Oz* in 1925 also. The screenplay was co-authored by Frank J. Baum and directed by Larry Semon, a popular comedian who also starred in the picture with Oliver Hardy (*before* his famous teaming with Stan Laurel!).

Wild plot liberties were taken and the resulting motion picture bore such slim resemblance to the original story that Ruth Plumly Thompson received countless angry letters from children expecting more! Though the film was a box-office failure, advertising postcards were issued and Bobbs-Merrill (which had obtained the *Wonderful Wizard of Oz* book rights after the Hill Company's 1902 bankruptcy) published a photo-play edition of the original story illustrated with eight black-and-white movie stills instead of color plates, and wrapped in a brightly graphic "movie edition" dust jacket. It was also about this time that the White and Wychoff Company marketed boxes of Oz stationery decorated with color drawings after both Denslow and Neill.

In the midst of this "Golden Age of Oz," Reilly & Lee revived the *Ozmapolitan* newspaper in 1926 in conjunction with the publication of Thompson's *The Hungry Tiger of Oz*. This, the twentieth Oz book, was promoted through plywood stand-ups of the Scarecrow for bookstore display. Using similar figures of the Patchwork Girl, *The Gnome King of Oz* was announced in 1927. A black-and-white version of the Land of Oz map was a Reilly & Lee coloring contest promotion in 1927, while the *Ozmapolitan* was again issued that year and in 1928 for *The Giant Horse of Oz*. In addition to distributing copies of the mock newspaper during this period, the publisher sponsored the first organized Oz appreciation society called the "Ozmite Club." Young enthusiasts received a small metal pin upon submitting their memberships and were privy to Oz club "secrets"!

Also in 1928, the New York based Jean Gros French Marionettes began touring the country with a musical adaptation of *Ozma of Oz* written by Ruth Plumly Thompson and entitled *The Magical Land of Oz*. To publicize the tour, small stiff-paper advertisements featuring the Scarecrow and Tin Woodman were handed out and the puppet presentation—with its fourteen-piece "Gnomes of Oz" orchestra—received a write-up in that year's *Ozmapolitan*.

The *Ozmapolitan* for 1928 was issued by Reilly & Lee in conjunction with Ruth Plumly Thompson's *The Giant Horse of Oz*. The four-page paper also included an article on the *Magical Land of Oz* marionette tour and made mention of the forthcoming Oz book for 1929, *Jack Pumpkinhead of Oz*. *Courtesy* The Baum Bugle.

A 15-inch plywood Patchwork Girl standee greeted bookstore customers eager to purchase *The Gnome King of Oz* in 1927. *Private collection.*

One of the earliest out-of-house Oz product endorsements occurred in 1929, when arrangements were made with Reilly & Lee to have several Oz characters promote the American Seating Company's school chairs. Ads appeared in educational journals, and a poster was issued featuring a stylized Patchwork Girl and Scarecrow modeling inappropriate seating posture! Meanwhile, a succession of Thompson Oz book titles followed with *Jack Pumpkinhead of Oz* (1929), *The Yellow Knight of Oz* (1930), *Pirates in Oz* (1931) and *The Purple Prince of Oz* (1932). By 1931, yet another minor film based on the Oz stories had been released as *The Land of Oz*. Later retitled *The Scarecrow of Oz*, the short feature starred California child talent maven Ethel Meglin's "Meglin Kiddies."

In 1932, a syndicated Oz comic page entitled "The Wonderland of Oz" appeared and was distributed by C.C Winningham, Inc. of Detroit. The strip was written and illustrated in black-and-white by Walt Spouse, closely following several of Baum's early Oz books. Although the feature ran daily Monday through Saturday, it only lasted into the following year. Reilly & Lee nevertheless provided newspaper offices with oversized Land of Oz maps and "Wonderland of Oz Scrapbooks" to be given out to young fans wishing to clip and mount the comic in book form. Oddly, the strips were later reprinted in color comic book format as part of the Funnies series published by Dell Publishing from 1938 to 1940. Reilly & Lee also took advantage of a picture puzzle fad that was currently sweeping the country by marketing two different boxed sets of die-cut puzzles in 1932. Identified as *Little Oz Books With Jig-Saw Puzzles*, each box included two booklets (each a reissue of one of the 1913 Little Wizard Series titles) and two picture puzzles.

The first animated version of *The Wizard of Oz* was completed in 1933 by Canadian Ted Eshbaugh. Though produced in Technicolor, legal difficulties made only a black-and-white version release possible. Also that year *Ojo in Oz* was published and, by special arrangement with Reilly & Lee, a "Wizard of Oz" radio program sponsored by Jell-O gelatin was broadcast over

To promote its company-sponsored "Wizard of Oz" radio program in 1933, Jell-O made special product counter displays which not only contained boxes of flavored gelatin, but also reminded patrons of the Oz program's weekly schedule. *Private collection.*

as many as twenty-six NBC affiliates every Monday, Wednesday and Friday from 5:45 to 6:00 P.M. The show starred the voices of child actress Nancy Kelly as Dorothy, Bill Adams as the Scarecrow, Parker Fennelly as the Tin Woodman and Jack Smart as the Cowardly Lion, with the entire cast assuming other roles as the narrative progressed through several Oz stories. As premiums for the show, which ran from September 25, 1933 to March 23, 1934, Reilly & Lee published four of the Little Wizard stories as booklets that included tempting Jell-O recipes. The program was further promoted through the press and Ozzy Jell-O counter display boxes.

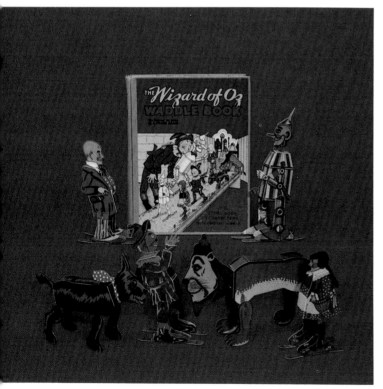

Blue Ribbon Books issued a toy edition of *The Wizard of Oz* in 1934, replete with full-color punchouts of six story characters designed to "waddle" down a yellow brick road incline as illustrated on the book's cover label. By comparison, Blue Ribbon's *Mickey Mouse Waddle Book* that was issued the same year contained just four such figures. *Waddles from private collection.*

In addition to Ruth Plumly Thompson's *Speedy in Oz* in 1934, Blue Ribbon Books, by arrangement with Bobbs-Merrill, published *The Wizard of Oz Waddle Book*. (The company concurrently marketed a similar *Mickey Mouse Waddle Book*.) This clever book and toy combination contained six die-cut punchouts of the story's main characters. Once properly assembled, the figures could shimmy or "waddle" down a yellow brick road ramp also furnished with the book.

The Wishing Horse of Oz was published in 1935 as was a portion of an original Oz manuscript written by Frank J. Baum entitled *The Laughing Dragon of Oz*. The latter story was illustrated in black-and-white by Milt Youngren and issued by Whitman Publishing Company as one of its popular Big-Little Books. The narrative had little in common with any of the previous Oz stories and when Whitman announced *The Enchanted Princess of Oz* as a sequel, their plans were upheld when Reilly & Lee brought suit.

After 1935 Reilly & Lee no longer printed color plates for any of its Oz books in order to minimize publishing expenses in the midst of the Great Depression. The series nevertheless continued the tradition of an annual title with Ruth Plumly Thompson's *Captain Salt in Oz* (1936), *Handy Mandy in Oz* (1937), *The Silver Princess of Oz* (1938) and *Ozoplaning with the Wizard of Oz* in 1939. Like L. Frank Baum, Thompson had, from the outset, realized the exploitation potential her characters held and tirelessly campaigned and cajoled Reilly & Lee in attempts to promote and merchandise her Oz books. The publisher, though, was largely ill-equipped to seriously consider her appeals and often discouraged or ignored her imaginative, yet unfeasible, proposals. Consequently, the authoress reluctantly chose to resign from the Oz series in 1940, weary after many years of creative differences with her publishers.

OVER THE RAINBOW

By 1939, the Oz stories and characters had firmly established themselves in the hearts and minds of the American public through the popularity of the Oz books and the intermittent novelties, festivals and promotions usually initiated by Reilly & Lee. However, perhaps not even L. Frank Baum could have envisioned the tremendous exposure his creations would receive as a result of the August, 1939 release of

Metro-Goldwyn-Mayer's lavish and costly Technicolor motion picture production of *The Wizard of Oz* starring Judy Garland. With a reception comparable only to that given the original 1902 stage production, the picture was a critical and popular success. It made its way on to a number of "ten best" lists that year and garnered two Academy Awards in addition to several other award nominations including that of "Best Picture" of 1939.

Just as it had done in actually creating the movie itself, MGM spared no expense when it came to promotion and reportedly spent $250,000 (an exorbitant amount at that time!) on a phenomenal advertising blitz that was detailed in an extravagantly illustrated campaign book distributed to theater owners for use in exploiting *The Wizard*. Among other things, the campaign offered promotional gimmicks such as Oz auto

An announcement for the Dart Board Equipment Company's *Wizard of Oz Dart Game* appeared in the September 1939 issue of the toy trade publication *Playthings*. Over fifty years later, company sales manager Sam Ervais recalled that fewer than one thousand such samples of the game were produced and distributed to department store chains nationwide. The company had hoped that a larger toy manufacturer might option the distribution rights to the Oz novelty. Mr. Ervais also remembered that Loew's Incorporated forwarded tickets to several company officials for the New York premiere of *The Wizard of Oz* at the city's Capitol Theater.

In their Christmas 1939 catalogue, Sears, Roebuck & Company advertised the L. Gidding Company's "Judy Garland dress." Included as a bonus with each dress order was a copy of Whitman's softcover *The Story of The Wizard of Oz. Courtesy Marge Meisinger.*

tire covers, bumper stickers, banners, flags, wall displays and life-sized cardboard cutouts of the movie characters. Also available were a variety of vivid and highly attractive promotional posters to be displayed in and around movie theaters showing the picture. The pressbook additionally boasted that *The Wizard*'s was "the biggest and most colorful advertising campaign ever put behind a motion picture" and that it would reach some "91,212,853...movie goers(!)" In the end, this proclamation proved not to be mere studio hype, due in part to the extraordinary amount of press coverage the film received through *Life, Look, Redbook, Cosmopolitan* and most other major publications of the day.

Loew's Incorporated, MGM's New York based parent company, established a royalty department to specifically handle *Wizard of Oz* merchandise accounts that would tie in with the film. *The Wizard*, though, was the company's first major venture into extensive merchandising, and actual licensing arrangements—including negotiations with Baum's widow, Maud—began much later than expected. Capitalizing on the familiarity of Oz, Loew's announced fifty-one pending accounts by summer 1939. Despite this,

many of the manufacturers who proposed Oz products did not actually obtain licenses or produce the goods after all. Some items were considered but probably never issued beyond prototypes or samples. These included wind-up toys by the Louis Marx Company; stuffed Cowardly Lion, Flying Monkey and "Toto the dog" dolls by Marie Hardy of New York; masquerade costumes by E. Simons & Sons; and a wide variety of Oz-inspired clothing, most of which was conceived to tie in with the name "Judy Garland" in accordance with her top billing as Dorothy. McLoughlin Brothers expressed interest in a *Wizard* coloring book, while Whitman had originally planned to offer a cutout book among the many other Oz paper items it produced. Similarly, the Ideal Novelty & Toy Company, which *did* market dolls of Judy Garland and "Strawman" Ray Bolger, had intended to issue a wood-jointed Tin Man doll as well.

Ideal Novelty & Toy Company's Judy Garland doll was flanked by likenesses of two of the actress's contemporaries in an ad for Spiegel's 1939 Christmas catalogue. Only the 15½-inch and 18-inch dolls were offered through catalogue mail-order. *Courtesy Marge Meisinger.*

To aid department stores in promoting the 1939 Christmas season, the W.L. Stensgaard Company offered a wide variety of *Wizard of Oz* display materials. Pictured above left is a hand-tinted photograph of a sample Oz show window complete with mechanically animated characters. At right is a salesman's advertising panel featuring drawings of similar (but stationary) figures, size listings for all display mannequins and a description of six mural-like paper decorations "including Witch and Monkey." The company stipulated that the full-length window setups would be exclusive to one store in each city. *Courtesy the late Dick Martin.*

Over the two years after the MGM movie's release, about thirty manufacturers followed through and actually purchased rights to market Oz tie-in products. These included an assortment of dolls, masks, toy soap figures, valentines, puzzles, stationery, mechanical store displays and even carpet sweepers. Also available were records and sheet music of the film's Oscar-winning score. Given the extensive publicity for the film and promotion by department stores, the movie tie-in merchandise had the potential to sell well. Yet in light of positive public response to Walt Disney's *Snow White and the Seven Dwarfs* two years earlier, it is likely that many toy companies were lured to the seemingly secure future promise of Max Fleischer's animated *Gulliver's Travels* (released in December, 1939) and Disney's *Pinocchio* (released in February, 1940).

In a time when motion picture production was fast and furious, *The Wizard of Oz* rarely played more than two weeks at most theaters. As a result, much of the Oz merchandise was quickly and cheaply made. Most was offered in five-and-dime stores nationwide, and was probably overshadowed by Disney and the usual Christmas fare of the impending holiday season. Once the film played out the last of the second- and third-run movie houses in 1940, manufacture of Oz movie-inspired products ceased.

For Valentine's Day 1940, Montgomery Ward offered an array of *Wizard of Oz* greeting cards. Although the ad claimed there were sixteen valentines in each boxed set, only twelve cards are known to exist, making it likely that several cards in the package were duplicates. *Courtesy Marge Meisinger.*

Aside from licensed manufacturers, a number of other companies sought to take advantage of the Oz awareness generated by the MGM film in 1939. Parker Brothers again reissued *The Wonderful Game of Oz* and it quickly became a top seller. Likewise, Rand McNally reprinted The Little Wizard Series in three volumes and published abridgements of six Baum Oz books, while Reilly & Lee issued "Popular Jumbo Editions" of *The Land of Oz*, *The Scarecrow of Oz* and *The Tin Woodman of Oz* on larger paper with redesigned covers. Since the MGM motion picture had, for the first time, provided Oz with widespread *international* exposure, various editions of the books—many of which contained illustrations heavily derived from the film's conceptions—also began cropping up in numerous foreign countries. When the picture opened in Great Britain (subject to censors deeming it too "frightening" for children!), a number of British photoplay editions appeared as did *The Wizard of Oz Card Game*.

Swift & Company's Oz-The Wonderful Peanut Spread was advertised via a full-page announcement in the *Detroit Times* for September 12, 1940. Available in two different sized glass jars and tin containers, the product name and characters were licensed by Loew's as an apparent tie-in with the recently released *Wizard of Oz* film. The original license expired on June 1, 1941, and by 1945 Swift had altered the product name to Oz-The Wonderful Peanut Butter. *Courtesy Bill Beem.*

NEW ADVENTURES IN OZ

By 1940, Oz illustrator extraordinaire John R. Neill had agreed to be Ruth Plumly Thompson's successor as the third "Royal Historian of Oz," contributing *The Wonder City of Oz* (1940), *The Scalawagons of Oz* (1941) and *Lucky Bucky in Oz* (1942) to the series. One charmingly nostalgic footnote to the latter title was the inclusion of an appeal printed on one dust jacket flap from the book's boy protagonist ("Bucky of Oz") for readers to purchase Victory Bonds and Stamps. By this time, though, excitement from the MGM film had waned and both Neill's untimely death in 1943 and World War II interrupted the Oz series. Consequently, very little Oz merchandise was produced during these lean years.

In 1944, however, Saalfield published an ingenious "animated" edition of *The Wizard of Oz* designed by Julian Wehr, who illustrated similar versions of *Alice in Wonderland* and *Puss in Boots*. By sliding paper tabs back and forth, the book's carefully articulated pictures could be made to move! Also that year, Bobbs-Merrill issued a "new" updated edition of *The Wizard of Oz* in which artist Evelyn Copelman's poignant paintings and ink drawings (greatly influenced by the 1939 movie) replaced the traditional Denslow illustrations for the first time in an unabridged edition, giving the story a more modern appearance.

The next few years continued on quietly with only the reissue of the MGM film songs in white wrappers and the publication of *The Magical Mimics of Oz* written by Baum historian Jack Snow (1905-1956) in 1946 and illustrated by Frank Kramer. Snow, flattered to have brought the series back from hiatus, was hopeful that Reilly & Lee would resume publication of an Oz book per year, yet disappointing sales made such plans unfeasible. In 1949, however, MGM *did* successfully re-release its *Wizard of Oz* movie with an updated (albeit largely scaled-down) publicity campaign that included revamped press and exploitation materials as well as a new assortment of theater posters and lobby display cards. With interest in Oz thus rejuvenated, Snow's *The Shaggy Man of Oz* was published, Capitol Records issued a *Dorothy and the Wizard in Oz* record set and the score of the 1939 film songs was reissued in several formats.

The early 1950s saw a number of children's *Wizard of Oz* and other Oz book adaptations and abridgements published by Random House, Little Golden Books and Wonder Books. In 1951 Reilly & Lee added another title to the Oz series with *The Hidden Valley of Oz* by Rachel R. Cosgrove (1922-   ) and illustrated by "Dirk" Gringhuis. Reilly & Lee next published Jack Snow's *Who's Who in Oz* in 1954. Though unsurpassed as reference for its biographical insight of over six hundred Oz characters, *Who's Who* sold poorly, perhaps because fans were disappointed that it wasn't a "real" Oz book.

MGM's *The Wizard of Oz* was re-released again in 1955, but this time less successfully and with only marginal profit. The following year, however, the film was leased to CBS Television for broadcast and, on November 3, 1956, an estimated forty-five million plus audience tuned in to be enchanted for two hours. This exceptional response prompted MGM Records to release *The Wizard* as one of the first soundtrack LP recordings composed of actual song and dialogue from a motion picture. (This soundtrack edition would later be offered as a 1961 product premium as well.) At this time also, the Lastic-Plastic Company issued a "Judy Garland as Dorothy" doll which proved to be an unflattering likeness of the actress.

The Sawyer Company advertised its new *Wonderful Wizard of Oz* View-Master packet for potential holiday gift-giving in the April 13, 1957 issue of *The Saturday Evening Post*.

CBS re-televised *The Wizard of Oz* again in 1959 to an even greater audience than the initial telecast. The film was shown every year thereafter by CBS through 1967, then by NBC-TV through 1975, and by CBS again from 1976 to the present. Thanks in large part to these annual television broadcasts, the story of *The Wizard of Oz* became increasingly familiar to Americans of all ages and, as a result, the Oz characters received additional product and merchandising exposure. Video Craft televised its series of 130 five-minute animated "Tales of the Wizard of Oz" cartoon shorts on Saturday mornings during the 1961-62 season and novelty items produced as tie-ins included coloring books and comic books, dolls, games, magic slates and Halloween costumes. In an unrelated promotion, Remco marketed an elaborate plastic "Showboat" theater for Christmas 1962, complete with script, scenery backdrops and small cardboard figures for four plays, *The Wizard of Oz* included. MGM Records reissued its movie soundtrack that same year in a special double-jacket format (available as such through the early 1980s) and the film's songbook also underwent revision.

1956 was also significant as the year that the *Wizard of Oz* book copyright expired, thereby allowing the story and its characters to become public domain. This opened up a whole new realm of potential merchandising, free from licensing and royalties. Within the next year several book adaptations—including comic books and coloring books—appeared as a result, as did the E.E. Fairchild Company's *The Wonderful Wizard of Oz Game*. In 1957, the Sawyer Company introduced a lovely three-reel View-Master packet faithfully recounting the original Oz story in twenty-one color frames.

The mid-1950s saw an extremely popular marketing tie-in through the Swift Company's Oz Peanut Butter. Swift had previously sold Oz-The Wonderful Peanut Spread in the early 1940s. The new promotion, however, featured decorated character product glasses, coloring books, recipe booklets and different sized decorated tins which could double as sand pails. The line prospered and continued into the 1960s before being briefly revived in limited areas in the 1970s.

Pictured is a circa 1950s Swift Oz Peanut Butter shipping box which contained the company's glass product tumblers.

The Artistic Toy Company took out full-page ads in toy trade publications to advertise its line of "Tales of the Wizard of Oz" dolls patterned after the 1961-62 cartoon program.

The *Ozmapolitan* children's newspaper was revived for the 1963 publication of *Merry Go Round in Oz. Courtesy* The Baum Bugle.

The following year, the Oz book series was revived for the first (and last *official*) time in twelve years with the 1963 publication of *Merry Go Round in Oz*. This, the fortieth Oz book, was written by the mother and daughter team of Eloise Jarvis McGraw (1915-   ) and Lauren McGraw Wagner (1944-   ), and featured illustrations by Oz and Baum historian Dick Martin (1927-1990). The book was advertised through the issuance of a two-color flyer, and was further publicized in a new issue of the *Ozmapolitan*.

On February 9, 1964, NBC presented Video Craft's animated *Return to Oz* musical, perhaps to challenge the annual CBS *Wizard of Oz* movie telecasts. The hour-long program was sponsored by the Housewares Division of General Electric and used Video Craft's "Tales of the Wizard of Oz" characters. Though the show was no match for MGM's *Wizard*, G.E. did issue a gold pot-metal charm bracelet to promote the broadcast, which was later repeated on February 21, 1965.

A Top Job product sample with a Proctor & Gamble *Wizard of Oz* premium puppet shrink-wrapped to the bottle, circa 1965.

Proctor & Gamble sponsored the 1965 telecast of *The Wizard of Oz* which the company promoted with a set of plastic-and-vinyl hand-puppets, free with the purchase of select products such as Oxydol, Top Job, Ivory Snow, Joy, and Zest. For proof-of-purchase and a quarter, eager fans could also send away for a cardboard Emerald

An oversized *Wizard of Oz* cardboard supermarket display was part of Proctor & Gamble's sponsorship for the 1969 telecast of the MGM film. The colorful presentation stood over five feet tall and included samples of the company's plastic hand-puppets, free to shoppers with the purchase of select products. *Courtesy Laura and Rickey Spann.*

The Homestead Mail Order Company's "Off to See the Wizard" wall decorations promised to "turn your child's room into a never-ending source of wonderment and joy" (1967). *Courtesy Michael Gessel.*

City theater, a script, and a Wizard puppet to complete the set of eight characters. This marketing promotion was repeated again in 1969 and was successful enough for the puppets to become one of the childhood staples of "baby boomers" nationwide!

Throughout the 1960s there was a steady trickle of Oz toys, puzzles, records and book adaptations. However, the second major wave of collected Oz merchandising to hit the American public with any impact since the 1939 film campaign occurred in the fall of 1967; not surprisingly, MGM was the driving force behind this resurgence. Having branched out into television production (becoming MGM-TV), the studio had begun researching the prospect of recycling a number of its *other* family-oriented

films for prime-time viewing much like the then-popular "Walt Disney's Wonderful World of Color." Building such programming around an Oz theme seemed like a logical means of drawing committed followers of the annual *Wizard* telecasts. The studio therefore felt it had found a viable project in a show that made its debut on ABC-TV on September 8, 1967 called "Off to See the Wizard."

The March, 1968 issue of *Toys and Novelties* introduced Deiner Industries' "Oz Jigglers," based on the animated characters from ABC-TV's "Off to See the Wizard."

Pictured is the paper label from the box which contained Mattel's 1967 "Off to See the Wizard" talking glove puppet.

Although "Off to See the Wizard" benefited from the creative efforts of veteran Oscar-winning animator Chuck Jones in addition to audience familiarity with the Oz characters and 1939 film songs, it lasted only through a single television season. This was probably due—at least in part—to the fact that fans were disappointed to find the animated Oz characters appearing in the hour-long show merely to open and close each episode. Despite this lack of success, industry insiders had anticipated otherwise for the series and a slew of manufacturers were licensed to produce "Off to See the Wizard" premiums, dolls, play figures, Halloween costumes, paint sets, puppets, and even decorated band-aids! Fortunately for many of the companies, their products could be marketed simply as "Wizard of Oz" tie-ins for several years after the show's cancellation.

In the fall of 1969, a low-budget, live-action matinee feature entitled *The Wonderful Land of Oz* was released through Cinetron Corporation. Though presented in "glowing, glorious storybook color" (as the movie ads and posters boasted), it was quickly forgotten. Within the next year, though, the growing Oz legend was given further sustenance when a Land of Oz theme park opened in Banner Elk, North Carolina. Among other things, the park offered a real yellow brick road which allowed visitors to walk through Dorothy's adventures in various Ozzy settings. The park displayed a number of costumes worn in the MGM Oz film and spawned its own souvenirs and memorabilia such as mugs, banners, T-shirts, and bumper stickers. After the attraction suffered a fire in 1976, the related merchandise was cheapened to include ordinary goods "made in Taiwan" and stamped only "The Land of Oz." Such measures reflected the park's troubled times before closing down after its 1980 season.

AN AMERICAN TRADITION

The Singer Sewing Machine Company sponsored the 1970 television broadcast of *The Wizard of Oz*. It was made especially poignant by Judy Garland's tragic death the previous year. The company pulled out all the stops in its promotion by reuniting surviving cast members Ray Bolger, Jack Haley, and Margaret Hamilton, and arranging numerous interviews with them for the media. There were also full-page magazine and newspaper ads ("Make a date to see SINGER

To promote its 1970 sponsorship of the twelfth annual telecast of *The Wizard of Oz*, the Singer Sewing Machine Company took out full-page ads such as this in magazines and newspapers nationwide. The ad shown here appeared in the March 14, 1970 issue of *TV Guide*.

of Dorothy), yet its theatrical release was unsuccessful and no tie-in products were manufactured. It wasn't until the film was sold to television several years later that a soundtrack record was issued as a product premium in 1980.

The Wiz, an all-black musical production of *The Wonderful Wizard of Oz*, began its Broadway run at the new Majestic Theater in New York City on January 5, 1975. This particular adaptation, which closely followed the plot of L. Frank Baum's original book, became a smash hit and went on to win a total of seven Tony Awards

An April 20, 1980 Sunday supplement advertised the *Journey Back to Oz* soundtrack album as a premium through the purchase of Texize products. Although Filmation had released the all-star animated feature film in 1974, television broadcasts prompted this record's release six years later. *Courtesy Cathi Dentler.*

Presents *The Wizard of Oz!*") in addition to a deal with MGM Merchandising for distribution of a free premium poster, a photo booklet illustrated with film stills, and the soundtrack record with a newly-designed jacket and specially reduced price. Despite this and subsequent telecasts, the film was also reissued to theaters that same year and again in 1972, as part of MGM's "Children's Matinee" series, with both revivals being advertised through new movie poster art and ad campaigns.

In 1974, Filmation released its full-length animated *Journey Back to Oz*, a project begun in 1962 as *Return to the Land of Oz* but delayed due to financial difficulties. The picture incorporated quality animation with many "star" voices (including that of Liza Minelli, "inheriting" the role including Best Musical of 1975, Best Score, Best Director, Best Choreography, Best Supporting Actor, Best Supporting Actress, and Best Costume Design. A two-color flyer was distributed to promote *The Wiz* and posters, T-shirts, and a souvenir program containing reprinted lyrics to some of the play's songs were among the items available for purchase by theater goers. Shortly after it opened, the score of the musical was published by Fox Fanfare Music, Inc., and Atlantic

interviews and the actors posed with their doll likenesses. The Mego line was extremely popular and, after slight revisions, the dolls were reissued later in the year accompanied by four Munchkin figures, a Munchkinland playset and, for Christmas 1975, a Witch's Castle playset available only through Sears. A second series of fifteen-inch dolls with vinyl heads and cloth bodies was manufactured and test-marketed in fifteen hundred sets, but never sold to the public.

The Mego Toy Corporation's line of plastic jointed *Wizard of Oz* dolls was offered with the *Witch's Castle Playset* in the 1975 Sears Christmas catalogue.

Records released an original cast album that would go on to win the 1976 Grammy Award for Best Cast Show Album.

The following February another Oz marketing blitz was initiated by the Mego Toy Corporation's introduction of its line of eight-inch poseable MGM *Wizard of Oz* dolls along with an Emerald City playset complete with a yellow brick road. Not surprisingly, preliminary marketing research for the dolls indicated an overwhelmingly high recognition of the characters by nursery school age children. The toys were given a royal sendoff via a New York press conference held at a screening of *The Wizard of Oz* in the grand ballroom of the Waldorf Astoria. Attenders Margaret Hamilton, Jack Haley, Ray Bolger and film producer Mervyn LeRoy granted extensive

Also in 1975, Marvel and DC Comics joined forces to produce an oversized comic book adaptation of MGM's *Wizard of Oz*. While faithful to the plot and "look" of the film, the book's awkward size made it difficult to stock, although it was later followed by a similar version of *The Land of Oz*. Both the Mego doll likenesses and the Marvel/DC comic artwork heavily influenced much of the Oz merchandise for several years to come. Marketed during the mid- to late-1970s were MGM movie-inspired items such as walking, spinning, and water-squirting(!) figures, Christmas ornaments, toiletries, trash cans, paper party goods, Halloween costumes, beach towels, sheets, and wallpaper.

Judy Garland's death, the subsequent and highly publicized 1970 auction of a pair of her ruby slippers, and the repeated telecasts of *The Wizard of Oz* were factors that gradually contributed to a shift in the film's status and how "Oz" was perceived by the American public. The movie had transcended from a fondly remembered annual treat to an integral part of popular culture of legendary proportions. Lending credence to this status was the historic impact made by Aljean Harmetz's brisk-selling 1977 book, *The Making of The Wizard of Oz*.

By this time only the fourteen Baum Oz book titles were available, published since 1959 by the Henry Regnery Company (although still bearing the Reilly & Lee imprint). With the other twenty-six titles out of print and obtainable only through libraries, the Oz book series inadvertently became distanced from the general public. Of course there were still coloring books, paper dolls, and other toy items inspired by the Baum characters geared toward children. However throughout the

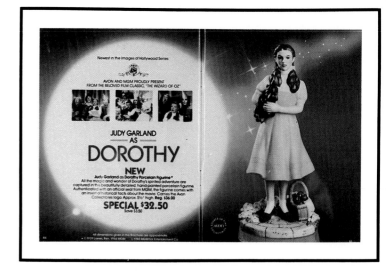

In 1985, a double-page Avon catalogue ad announced the addition of a fifth porcelain figurine to the company's Images of Hollywood Series.

All eight of the Knowles limited edition *Wizard of Oz* collector plates (first introduced in 1977) had appreciated in value by 1984, as was proudly announced in this Bradford Exchange advertisement.

In 1984, Effanbee produced "Judy Garland as Dorothy" as sixth in its series of Hollywood "legend" dolls. Ads for the doll heightened desirability by quoting an "Entertainment Tonight" poll which placed the original 1939 Ideal doll at the top of the list of most wanted celebrity dolls.

34

1960s and (especially) the 1970s, the *Wizard of Oz* telecasts made the MGM characters, dialogue, and songs increasingly familiar to millions of people who grew up never missing a single broadcast. When many of these people became adults, they could afford to create a demand for "quality" reminders of the charm the movie held for them.

The trend toward issuing fine collectibles, collector's items, and "investibles" was given impetus through the Edwin M. Knowles China Company's series of eight limited edition collector plates introduced in 1977 in anticipation of the film's fortieth anniversary. The series enjoyed great success and gave *The Wizard of Oz* the distinction of becoming the first motion picture to be honored by a commemorative plate collection—a practice now commonplace. Not surprisingly, other finely crafted collectibles including limited edition prints, porcelain figures, music boxes and dolls followed into the 1980s.

The film version of Broadway's *The Wiz* was released in 1978 starring Diana Ross (as a twenty-four-year-old Dorothy!) and Michael Jackson. Despite high energy and spirit, the movie otherwise seemed to share little in common with the Oz everyone knew and loved, including the musical that inspired it. Although a handful of licensees for *The Wiz* were listed in the film's pressbook, the only items believed to have been marketed were a soundtrack album, a songbook, a calendar, a making-of-the-movie book, a movie edition book (actually the text of *The Wonderful Wizard of Oz* illustrated with stills) and, oddly enough, a View-Master packet. Meanwhile, plans for other tie-ins such as costumes and masks, girls' disco clothing, comic books, and men's, women's, and children's sportswear, were probably never realized.

Another disappointing film venture was Disney's *Return to Oz* in 1985. An amalgam of *The Land of Oz* and *Ozma of Oz*, the film took great pains to remain literal to Baum (versus MGM's conceptions), but the resulting experience was solemn and dismal, lacking in the simple fun it so desperately needed more of. Prior to its release, expectations for the new Oz picture were at an all-time high since 1939. Directed by Oscar winner Walter Murch, the film was backed by a $25 million budget bolstered by an expansive multimillion dollar media merchandising and advertising campaign. Promotions encompassed a broad scope of publicity gimmicks and contests

Smucker's Preserves made three *Return to Oz* hand-puppets available as premiums throughout the summer of 1985.

(including Disneyworld vacations), a national Waldenbooks chain tie-in, a *Return to Oz* traveling department store "road show" supplemented by authentic movie costumes and props, and a gala June 16, 1985 Radio City Music Hall world premiere.

Although *Return to Oz* failed to appeal to the American public overall, it was popular and well-received in several foreign countries, Japan in particular. This led a number of overseas merchants to produce a variety of unique tie-in items not found in the United States. Given the tremendous media hype, many American manufacturers had been primed for positive and enthusiastic acceptance of the Disney film and released calendars, puzzles, games, books of all kinds, paper dolls, puppets, and records. In lieu of the movie's lukewarm reception, some of the novelties lingered in stores and supermarkets for years afterwards with overstock eventually being remaindered to wholesale outlets.

The Franklin Mint was one of the first collectibles companies to anticipate the fiftieth anniversary of MGM's *The Wizard of Oz* when it marketed its "Judy Garland as Dorothy" doll in 1987. This particular advertisement suggested the doll as a gift-giving idea for the 1988 holiday season. *Courtesy The Franklin Mint.*

Perhaps no one could have predicted the overwhelming impact made on the toy and collectibles marketplace as a result of the 1989 Oz film anniversary. In its listing of official *Wizard of Oz* fiftieth anniversary licensees, Turner Entertainment Company (which had acquired the rights to the movie upon purchasing a substantial portion of the MGM film library) announced over fifty manufacturers and merchants interested in producing Oz-related goods! Even more astounding was the fact that most of the licensees did actually follow through

The premiere issue in The Hamilton Collection's first series of *Wizard of Oz* fiftieth anniversary commemorative plates was advertised extensively in magazines and newspapers beginning in 1988.

A TIMELESS CLASSIC

After *Return to Oz*, the Oz merchandise market was relatively dormant until a number of quality collectibles companies started to anticipate the impending 1989 fiftieth anniversary of MGM's *The Wizard of Oz*. As early as 1986, The Franklin Mint began advertising its porcelain "Judy Garland as Dorothy" Heirloom Collector's doll. Shortly thereafter, the company introduced many other fine Oz collector's items, a line to which it added into the early 1990s.

with their plans, many of which included entire lines of diverse products. Very little anticipated merchandise went unproduced, and those things that did not materialize included a comic book, a series of color prints depicting movie scenes, and several small toy items such as a soap-making kit, "scribble" pads, coin purses, diaries, a "play-lite" picture kit, and figural button-on and clip-on characters. The majority of unrealized merchandise was to have been issued by the

Multi Toys Corporation of Cresskill, New Jersey. Even so, the company's vast array of other Oz products contributed substantially to what seemed like an endless barrage of dolls in all sizes, toys of every description, figurines, books, plates, Christmas ornaments, music boxes, and medallions. Never before had there been such an extraordinary deluge of Oz merchandise available, with a wealth of offerings running the gamut from one dollar for a coloring book to three *million* dollars for a pair of jeweler Harry Winston's *real* ruby slippers!

Also in 1989, MGM/UA Home Video issued a special "limited edition" commemorative version of the *Wizard of Oz* videotape (first released in 1980) backed by an impressive $8.5 million promotional campaign that helped make it one of the ten top-selling video titles of the year. Meanwhile, the film itself was released once again to theaters for several limited engagements in major cities across the country.

Among the many *Wizard of Oz* items planned for production by the Multi Toys Corporation in 1988 were six different "Munchkin" hand-puppets. Although the company *did* follow through in manufacturing similar puppets of the main characters, production of these secondary characters was halted early on, with existing limited quantities being remaindered to toy stores in Canada. (The packaging for known examples appears in both English and French.) In addition to the puppets shown, a Lollipop Guild Boy and Munchkin Woman were part of the ill-fated set of six.

For the fiftieth anniversary of two of the most popular films of all time, Turner Home Entertainment issued a special booklet previewing the merchandising exploitation both movies would receive to mark the occasion.

Turner Home Entertainment
Presents

A Fiftieth Anniversary Tribute To
GONE WITH THE WIND
and
THE WIZARD OF OZ

DowBrands distributed a full-color flyer early in 1989 via Sunday newspapers across the country in order to endorse its various food storage bags and wraps as well as the company's *Wizard of Oz* placemat offer.

Adding further fuel to the fire of the widespread "Ozmania" were countless Oz celebrations and festivities held throughout the year. Among the most spectacular of these revelries was a nearly month-long series of events sponsored by New York's Macy's department store. It featured decorative displays of extravagantly costumed mannequins and salespeople, a Guiness World Record-breaking tap dance, costume contests, puppet shows, musical revues, and larger-than-life Oz character balloon marquees—all providing an affectionate coronation for the well-loved film. In addition, Macy's marketed exclusive "Oz Time" watches and designer clothing for the occasion. About this same time, a magnificent "theater in the round" arena production of *The Wizard of Oz* began touring the country via performances in some seventy cities. Backed by corporate sponsors Purina Dog Chow and Downy Fabric Softener, the musical extravaganza benefited from a comprehensive publicity campaign and it, too, offered its own extensive line of trinkets, tokens, and souvenirs.

Even though the heightened frenzy surrounding the MGM film's fiftieth anniversary has since subsided, the resulting jubilation underscores the acknowledgement that L. Frank Baum's story and characters have reached yet another plateau that is probably more than the "Dreamer of Oz" himself could have imagined: unequivocal immortality. Given the phenomenal longevity and the ever-burgeoning interest for all things Oz, it is safe to assume that Baum's vision will forever stay fresh and exciting to the young at heart who remain devoted to its simple charms. The "staying power" of *The Wizard of Oz* and its mystical ability to hold children of all ages spellbound reminds us of its humble beginnings over ninety years ago through the writings of a warm, gentle-hearted man and his dream of creating that enchanted land that surely lies somewhere "over the rainbow" for the believer in us all!

"It's Oz Time At Macy's!" was the slogan used to promote the department store's "Oz-some" *Wizard of Oz* fiftieth anniversary extravaganza during August and September of 1989. In pulling out all the stops to celebrate the momentous occasion, Macy's offered its own exclusive "Oz Time" wristwatch, the face of which was shown on this advertising poster.

Autographs

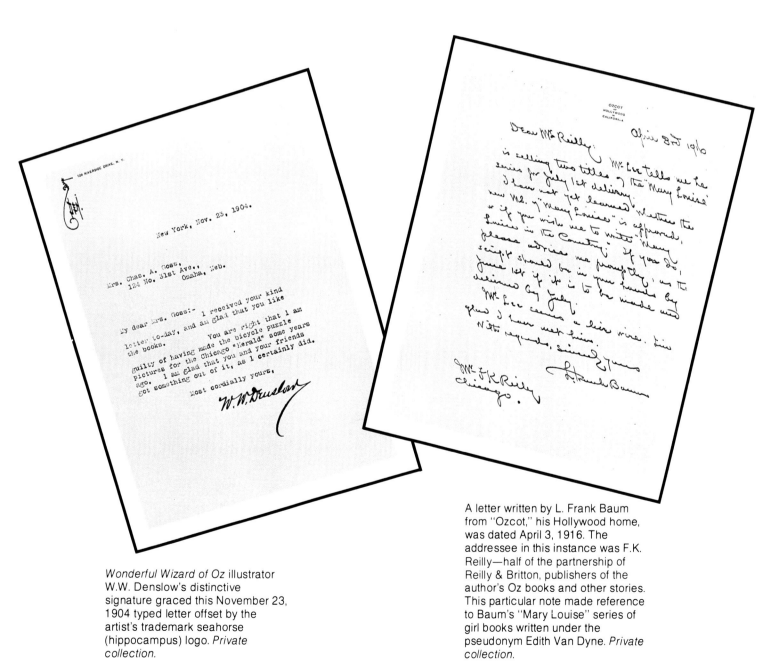

Wonderful Wizard of Oz illustrator W.W. Denslow's distinctive signature graced this November 23, 1904 typed letter offset by the artist's trademark seahorse (hippocampus) logo. *Private collection.*

A letter written by L. Frank Baum from "Ozcot," his Hollywood home, was dated April 3, 1916. The addressee in this instance was F.K. Reilly—half of the partnership of Reilly & Britton, publishers of the author's Oz books and other stories. This particular note made reference to Baum's "Mary Louise" series of girl books written under the pseudonym Edith Van Dyne. *Private collection.*

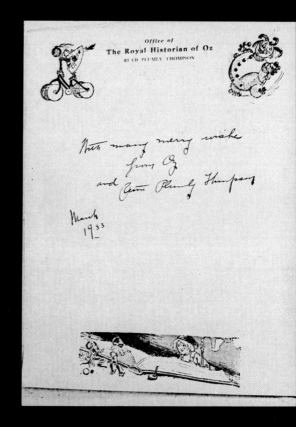

A personal letter from long-time Oz book illustrator John R. Neill was hand written to Oz book authoress Ruth Plumly Thompson and dated May 20, 1936. In it Neill remained optimistic that Thompson would write another Oz book for 1937. She would, in fact, add three more titles to the series before retiring after the publication of her nineteenth Oz book in 1939, at which time Neill himself tried his hand at illustrating *and* writing the series. *Private collection.*

A March, 1933 inscription from the second Royal Historian of Oz to an admirer of her stories was inscribed, "With many merry wishes from Oz and Ruth Plumly Thompson" on the writer's special Oz stationery. Thompson usually only signed her correspondence as "Ruth" or simply "R.P.T." *Private collection.*

Actor Fred Stone, the "original" Scarecrow from the 1902 *Wizard of Oz* stage play, signed salutations to "Richard" in this 1940s inscription. *Courtesy Tom and Eileen Bonawitz; photo: Eileen Bonawitz.*

A scene still from the reckless 1925 Chadwick Pictures silent film version of *The Wizard of Oz* as autographed by many of the production's featured players. From left to right the signatures read: "Babe" Oliver Hardy (the Tin Woodman), signing both his nickname and stage name; Dorothy Dwan (Dorothy), wife of director and comedic star Larry Semon (the Scarecrow); Bryant Washburn (Prince Kynde); Charlie Murray (the Wizard), a veteran of Keystone comedies; Josef Swickard (the Prime Minister); and Otto Lederer (Ambassador Wikked). *Courtesy Camden House Auctioneers.*

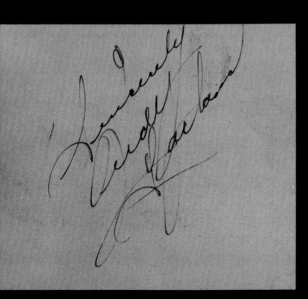

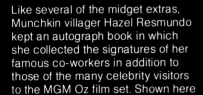

Like several of the midget extras, Munchkin villager Hazel Resmundo kept an autograph book in which she collected the signatures of her famous co-workers in addition to those of the many celebrity visitors to the MGM Oz film set. Shown here

A circa 1960s Judy Garland autograph was signed in ball-point pen on a picture of the actress from her most memorable screen role. *Courtesy Cordelia and Thomas Platt.*

A circa late-1930s portrait of a debonair Jack Haley—sans his silver "Tin Man" wardrobe—as inscribed by the popular entertainer. *Courtesy Tod Machin; photo: JoAnn Groves.*

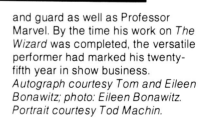

"Wizard" Frank Morgan's portrait and bold signature. The actor received his Oz assignment in lieu of such worthy contenders as Ed Wynn, Wallace Beery, and W.C. Fields. In addition to playing the pivotal title character in the 1939 movie, Morgan was featured as Emerald City gatekeeper, cabby, and guard as well as Professor Marvel. By the time his work on *The Wizard* was completed, the versatile performer had marked his twenty-fifth year in show business. *Autograph courtesy Tom and Eileen Bonawitz; photo: Eileen Bonawitz. Portrait courtesy Tod Machin.*

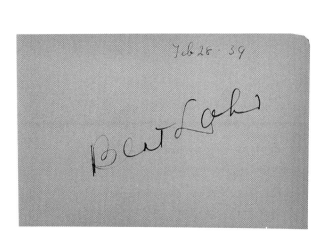

A Bert Lahr signature, signed on a fan's autograph book page, was dated February 28, 1939—only days after the comedian completed principal photography as the Cowardly Lion in *The Wizard of Oz*. Also shown is a late-1930s portrait of the actor. *Portrait courtesy Tod Machin.*

Throughout the latter part of his career, Ray Bolger was routinely inundated with autograph requests from fans who fondly recalled his *Oz* performance. To keep pace with the demand, he kept a supply of movie scene stills on hand which he usually co-signed as "The Scarecrow of Oz."

A circa 1940 publicity portrait of dancer Ray Bolger was signed to midwest theater owner Bill Holden. The inscription read: "To Bill Holden: Aw. What the hell! I'll cut. But not more than 30 seconds. Sincerest regards—Ray Bolger." *Courtesy Tod Machin; photo: JoAnn Groves.*

Warm greetings from the Wicked Witch to Hazel Resmundo read: "Merry Christmas Hazel & the best of wishes! From 'Mag the Hag'— Margaret Hamilton." This particular inscription reflected Hamilton's good-natured acceptance of the ribbing she received from cast and crew due to her horrific getup! *Courtesy Tod Machin; photo: JoAnn Groves.*

Akin to Ray Bolger's happy plight, Margaret Hamilton was increasingly deluged with fan mail and autograph requests as *The Wizard of Oz* heightened in popularity throughout the 1970s and 1980s. The actress frequently signed her full name, her nickname "Maggie" and "WWW," short for Wicked Witch of the West—the role with which she was indelibly linked.

Another Billie Burke autograph as signed in Munchkin Hazel Resmundo's keepsake book. *Courtesy Tod Machin; photo: JoAnn Groves.*

"To Hazel with love, Billie Burke, 1938" read the inscription on a photograph of Florenz Ziegfeld's widow—whose alter-ego at the time of this signature was Glinda, the Good Witch of the North. *Courtesy Tod Machin; photo: JoAnn Groves.*

Hollywood dog trainer Carl Spitz autographed publicity photos of two of his most famous canines to theater owner Bill Holden circa 1940. Both pictures were "co-signed" by the dogs themselves with inked paw prints. The portrait at right read: "Many thanks by Carl Spitz and Toto to Mr. Bill Holden." The photo below was inscribed: "To Bill Holden. Toto, Mr. Binkie, Carl Spitz." (The Scottish terrier Mr. Binkie starred with Ronald Coleman in 1939's *The Light That Failed*.) *Courtesy Tod Machin; photo: JoAnn Groves.*

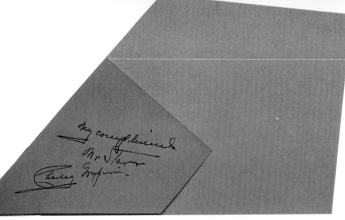

A signature and publicity portrait of veteran character actor Charley Grapewin. As associate producer Arthur Freed's first choice to play Dorothy's Uncle Henry in the MGM Oz film, Grapewin postponed his retirement from the screen to fulfill the role. The part called for one week's work at a salary of $750. *Autograph courtesy Tom and Eileen Bonawitz; photo: Eileen Bonawitz. Portrait courtesy Tod Machin.*

Seventeen of the original 124 *Oz* midget actors autographed this Munchkin photo in 1989. *Courtesy Tom and Eileen Bonawitz; photo: Eileen Bonawitz.*

SHELTON APARTMENTS
1735 NORTH WILCOX AVENUE
HOLLYWOOD CALIFORNIA

HOLLYWOOD 7-3141

Dear Cal:-

You are right. I have never had the demanding ego that afflicts the stars of our industry. You don't receive a lot of glory playing Mothers and Aunts and Gossips. But now that I am compelled to look back on my movie memories and my eventful week shooting OZ, I was a bit bruised by the brushing off I received compared to Charley. He had a less significant "role" in the scheme of things and received no more money. I had appeared with him before and we were always a "good fit". He was a little embarrassed by the slight to me, especially when the feature ran that deemed me "Clara XXXXXXX Blandish." That did make me cross. I am, in addition to everything, proud of the family name. My father owned and commanded the Willard-Mudgett and we were related from a distance to Howard Greeley.

Have you settled with the lawyers yet? I expected to hear one way or the other by now. I hope that whatever you get will make the years less burdensome. We can't hold back the clock, but we should have the wherewithal to keep it in good repair. Let me know. I am interested and rooting for you.

Yours affectionately,

Clara Blandick

A July 31, 1941 signed letter from "Auntie Em" Clara Blandick to a friend described some bitterness felt by the actress. She claimed to have been "a bit bruised" at the apparent slighting she received with respect to her work in *The Wizard of Oz* in addition to being given a botched billing on at least one occasion. *Courtesy Tom and Eileen Bonawitz.*

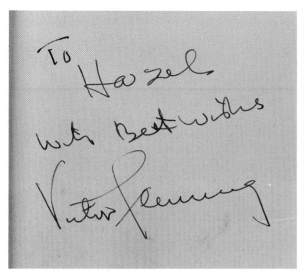

Respected and accomplished as director of such Hollywood productions as *Test Pilot*, *Treasure Island*, *Captains Courageous*, *Gone With the Wind*, and *The Wizard of Oz*, Victor Fleming signed Hazel Resmundo's autograph book in 1938. *Courtesy Tod Machin; photo: JoAnn Groves.*

In 1938, "wunderkind" costume designer Gilbert Adrian co-signed this autograph page from the Resmundo book with his fiancée, actress Janet Gaynor, whom he would marry in August 1939. (The yet unwed couple was photographed lunching by eager paparazzi earlier that year.) Revered as couturier for glamorous ladies such as Joan Crawford, Norma Shearer, Hedy Lamarr, and Gaynor, Adrian capably accepted the challenge of inventing an infinite variety of wardrobe for the imaginary denizens of Oz. *Autographs courtesy Tod Machin; photo: JoAnn Groves.*

Veteran actor Buddy Ebsen began filming *The Wizard of Oz* in 1938 when he was cast as the Tin Woodman. Although a severe allergic reaction to the aluminum makeup used to powder his face forced Ebsen to withdraw from the picture altogether, the actor acknowledged his brief contribution by signing this film scene (in which he appears in his forfeited role) during the early 1980s.

A signed portrait of distinguished producer Mervyn LeRoy, who realized a boyhood dream in overseeing the 1938-39 creative efforts that brought MGM's *The Wizard of Oz* to life. *Courtesy Tom and Eileen Bonawitz.*

Each of the two thousand limited edition *Wizard of Oz* prints (24" x 30") produced by The Nostalgia Merchant in 1977 were individually numbered and personally signed by "Scarecrow" Ray Bolger and "Tin Man" Jack Haley.

A publicity flyer for the December 10, 1990 broadcast of the made-for-television movie *The Dreamer of Oz* was autographed by star John Ritter "For Tom, Best Ozways—L. Frank John Ritter." *Courtesy Tom and Eileen Bonawitz.*

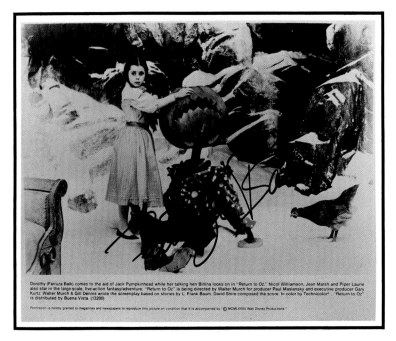

Dorothy (Fairuza Balk) comes to the aid of Jack Pumpkinhead while her talking hen Billina looks on in "Return to Oz." Nicol Williamson, Jean Marsh and Piper Laurie also star in the large-scale, live-action fantasy/adventure. "Return to Oz" is being directed by Walter Murch for producer Paul Maslansky and executive producer Gary Kurtz. Walter Murch & Gill Dennis wrote the screenplay based on stories by L. Frank Baum. David Shire composed the score. In color by Technicolor® , "Return to Oz" is distributed by Buena Vista. (13200)

Permission is hereby granted to magazines and newspapers to reproduce this picture on condition that it is accompanied by © MCMLXXXV Walt Disney Productions."

Fairuza Balk's signature as it appeared on a scene still from Walt Disney's *Return to Oz* (1985) in which the Canadian child actress portrayed Dorothy Gale. *Courtesy Tom and Eileen Bonawitz; photo: Eileen Bonawitz.*

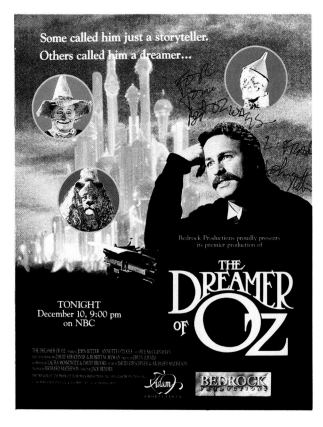

Books and Booklets

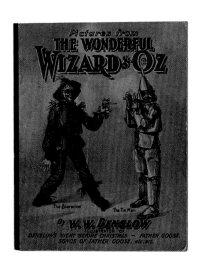

Pictures From The Wonderful Wizard of Oz was published circa 1903 by George W. Ogilvie & Company in Chicago. The booklet reprinted twenty-two of the twenty-four *Wonderful Wizard* color book plates combined with an original story fabricated by Thomas H. Russell to accompany the illustrations, which were intentionally printed out of sequence. Ogilvie acquired uncut sheets of W.W. Denslow's color plates when George M. Hill, the first publisher, went bankrupt in 1902. The color lithographed cover depicting Fred Stone and Dave Montgomery was derived from publicity stills taken for the Oz musical's 1902 Chicago opening.

In *Denslow's Scarecrow and The Tin-man* (1904, G.W. Dillingham), the illustrator detailed the comic dilemmas encountered when the two stage personalities eloped from the Majestic Theater in New York between performances of *The Wizard of Oz. Courtesy Michael Patrick Hearn.*

The 1925 Chadwick Pictures photoplay edition of *The Wizard of Oz* as published by Bobbs-Merrill featured star Larry Semon as the Scarecrow on the dust wrapper cover. On one of the jacket flaps, the most celebrated ''Scarecrow'' at that time, Fred Stone, wrote a brief letter to his ''little friends'' which originally appeared as the preface to a 1920s edition of the book. In the note's text, Stone made reference to having named his own daughter ''Dorothy'' after the *Wizard*'s heroine (left). In place of color plates, the book was illustrated with eight black-and-white movie stills (right). *Courtesy Blair Frodelius.*

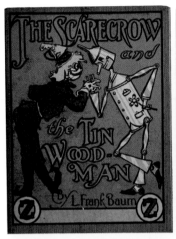

The Wizard of Oz Waddle Book was published in 1934 by Blue Ribbon Books through special arrangement with Bobbs-Merrill. The book contained six die-cut character punchouts, a yellow brick road runway and assembly instructions bound in at the end of the text. Some later Bobbs-Merrill printings of *The Wizard* inadvertently retained notice of the waddle instructions on the book's title page. Very few copies of the *Waddle Book* are known to exist from which the owners resisted removing the waddles!

In promotion of the "Wizard of Oz" radio program in 1933 and 1934, four of Baum's 1913 Little Wizard stories were reprinted. The booklets were obtainable by mailing Jell-O package fronts to the company's Battle Creek, Michigan offices. Each pamphlet contained Ozzy gelatin recipes and featured the Scarecrow and Tin Woodman carrying a large platter of Jell-O on the back cover—subtle advertisement for the radio show's sponsor!

Whitman's popular series of "Big-Little Books" included this 425-page volume written by L. Frank Baum's eldest son, Frank J. Baum, and copyrighted 1934 (though published in January 1935). Typical of each book's format, nearly every other page of *The Laughing Dragon of Oz* featured a black-and-white drawing by Milt Youngren.

Bobbs-Merrill's 1939 edition of *The Wizard of Oz* featured sepia-tone endpapers illustrated with movie stills, a new "Read-the-Book-and-See-the-Movie" dust wrapper and "the complete text on which the famous Metro-Goldwyn-Mayer movie" was based—all this for only $1.19! (Interestingly, the very first copies of this book's dust jacket misspelled the middle part of the film studio's name as "Goldwin.")

Whitman's *The Wizard of Oz Paint Book* (1939) featured a brief narrative based on Baum's text accompanied by large line drawings of characters somewhat similar to their MGM screen counterparts as illustrated by Henry E. Vallely.

Henry E. Vallely's drawings for Whitman's *Oz Paint Book* were incorporated, along with a slightly abridged text, into *The Story of The Wizard of Oz*. This softcover book was later issued in a reduced format "with pictures to color" as a Cocomalt drink premium. Copies were also issued free with the purchase of a "Judy Garland dress" through Sears, Roebuck & Company at Christmas 1939.

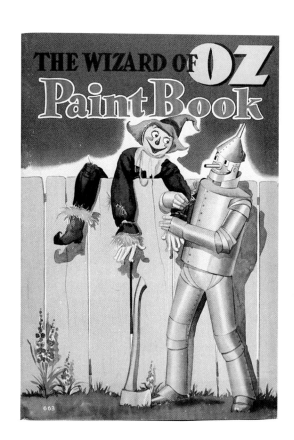

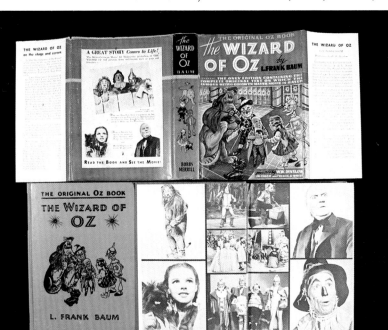

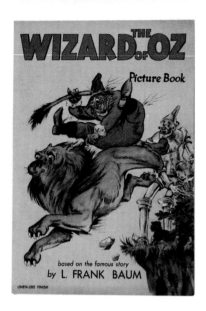

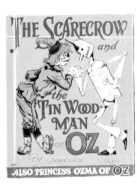

The Wizard of Oz Picturebook was also published by Whitman in 1939. In just twelve "linen-like" pages, artist "Leason" provided a wildly comic, action-packed abridgement of "the famous story by L. Frank Baum."

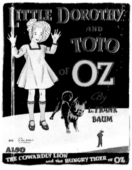

Grossett & Dunlap printed this *Wizard* abridgement in 1939 to coincide with the release of the MGM film. Pictured below the book is the dust wrapper's rear panel. In the jacket's flap synopsis, the publisher advised that "...you will want to own this beautiful book to read and re-read long after the movie is gone."

Jumping on the 1939 Oz publicity bandwagon, publisher Rand McNally printed an assortment of nine hardcover Oz books uniform in size and retailing for a paltry ten cents each. The set included Baum's six Little Wizard stories from 1913—reprinted two to a volume—and abridged "Junior Editions" of six of the author's popular full-length Oz books. The entire series was also sold as a vividly boxed set. *Book box courtesy Tod Machin; photo: JoAnn Groves.*

An unabridged "photoplay" edition of *The Wizard of Oz* was issued in early 1940 by the British publisher Hutchinson. The book was embellished with eight "coloured" movie stills in addition to a wraparound cover scene from the film which was repeated on the dust jacket. This edition was also printed in a plain cloth binding with a different movie-based jacket picturing the confrontation with the Cowardly Lion. According to the book's dust wrapper flap, Hutchinson had also proposed a *Wizard of Oz Painting Book* and an Oz movie cutout book.

Wizard of Oz Story Book was the least expensive of the 1940 Hutchinson titles printed in Great Britain. This paperback featured a number of Denslow-inspired line drawings in addition to promoting the "£ 750,000 MGM Coloured Film" on its cover. Curiously enough, all of the Hutchinson abridgements mentioned W.W. Denslow's illustrations but none credited Baum as author!

Wizard of Oz was a hardcover abridgement of Baum's story illustrated with two hand-tinted stills from the MGM film as well as a number of line drawings after Denslow's work. It was published by Hutchinson in Great Britain in 1940.

Another Oz title issued by Hutchinson to tie in with the 1940 English release of MGM's *The Wizard of Oz* was this "colouring book" with drawings based on Denslow's original artwork. Each picture was printed in black-and-white opposite an identical color sample to be used as a guide.

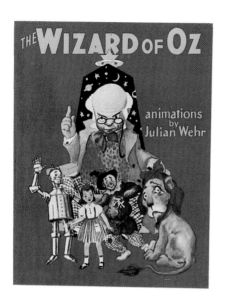

Artist and paper engineer Julian Wehr designed this *Wizard* adaptation for the Saalfield Publishing Company in 1944. The spiral-bound book was sold in a matching dust jacket and six of its twenty-four pages contained skillfully articulated illustrations which, for example, enabled Dorothy to oil the Tin Man or the Wizard to fill the Scarecrow's head with brains.

Denslow's Scarecrow and The Tin-Man was reprinted in 1946 by Perks Publishing with line drawings after the Denslow originals by Mary and Wallace Stover. The pamphlet's cover art was taken directly from the 1904 compilation *Denslow's Scarecrow and The Tin-Man and Other Stories.* Earliest printings of the booklet identified New York as place of publication, with pictures in black-and-yellow. Later editions, however, were marked Silver Springs, Maryland, with pictures in black-and-yellow and black-and-blue.

Three of L. Frank Baum's Oz stories were adapted for the Little Golden Book series beginning in 1951 with *The Road to Oz. The Emerald City of Oz* and *The Tin Woodman of Oz* were both published in 1952. Each book was also printed with special cloth bindings for libraries.

In 1944 Bobbs-Merrill consigned Evelyn Copelman to provide the original *Wizard of Oz* text with new illustrations, replacing W.W. Denslow's famous drawings for the first time in an unabridged edition of the book. Her fine watercolor and pen-and-ink pictures (largely patterned after MGM movie stills) gave the story a fresh, updated appearance. (Copelman would also illustrate a 1947 Bobbs-Merrill edition of Baum's *The Magical Monarch of Mo*.) Over the years, this version of *The Wizard* was reissued in countless formats (some with additional pictures), and has remained in print to this day.

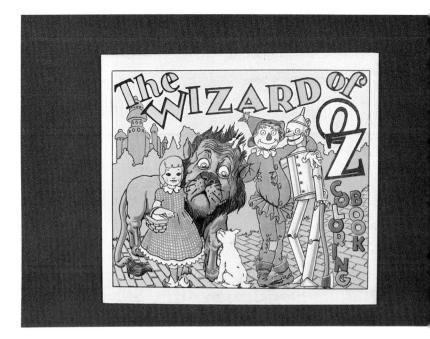

Swift & Company's *Wizard of Oz Coloring Book* was printed in March 1955. Its ten pages advertised the company's Oz Peanut Butter while briefly recounting the original Baum story.

One of the most enduring adaptations of *The Wizard of Oz* was the 1950 storybook published by Random House. Although it was reprinted many times up through the 1970s (including a sturdy library binding version), the earliest editions pictured Dorothy and the Guardian of the Gates on the back cover.

The Wizard of Oz as published in 1951 by Wonder Books followed the original story closely. First editions of this version were copiously illustrated in forty-two pages. The book was later edited to twenty pages and was available in that format into the early 1980s (left). Another Wonder Books adaptation published in 1956 focused entirely on the *Cowardly Lion* chapter from the original book (right).

The Wizard was issued as one of Junior Deluxe's classic books and story collections in 1955 and remained in print through the late 1960s. Pictured with the book is a 1960s edition dust jacket.

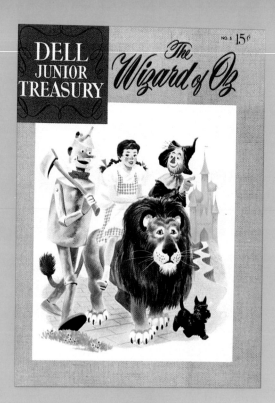

Dell Treasury Comics published their comic book edition of *The Wizard of Oz* in 1956. The comic's script writer, Gaylord Dubois, wrote the text for this and over three thousand other comic book titles in his forty year career.

Saalfield's 1957 *Wizard of Oz Coloring Book* was another abridgement that closely portrayed the characters and events in the original story.

Number 535 in the Classics Illustrated Junior series, this comic book *Wizard* was printed in 1957. The earliest copies list other available titles up to number 534 on the back cover. A great number of foreign language editions have appeared since the comic's original publication, including translations in Danish, Dutch, Spanish, Finnish, French, German, Norwegian and Swedish.

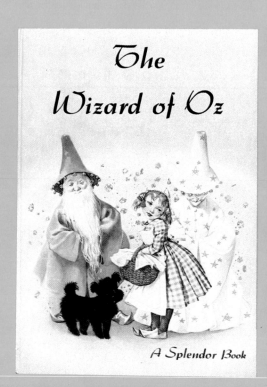

This abridged edition of *The Wizard of Oz* was first published in Italy in 1957 as *Il Mago di Oz*. Notable for Maraja's beautiful illustrations, the book was printed in the United States in 1958 by both Grossett & Dunlap and Duell, Sloan & Pearce (above). The Grossett & Dunlap edition was reissued in 1986.

An abridged version of *The Wizard of Oz* appeared in 1957 as one of Whitman Publishing's series of illustrated classics (left). In 1965, it was reprinted with a new cover design (right).

To promote its Oz Peanut Butter, Swift & Company distributed this fold-out booklet circa the early 1960s. It featured "wonderful recipes" including such treats as "Aunt Em's Peanut Butter Apple Pie," "Tin Woodman's Sundae," and "Dorothy's Peanut Butter Cake."

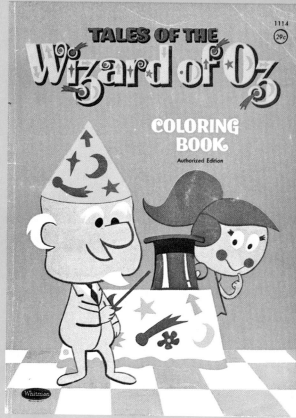

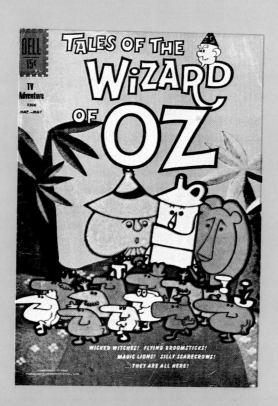

Videocraft's animated "Tales of the Wizard of Oz" television characters were the inspiration for an "authorized edition" coloring book published by Whitman in 1962. *Courtesy Hake's Americana & Collectibles, York, Pa.*

Dell's *Tales of the Wizard of Oz* comic book (dated March-May 1962) took alarming and often bizarre liberties in manipulating the Oz cartoon characters through extraordinary plots.

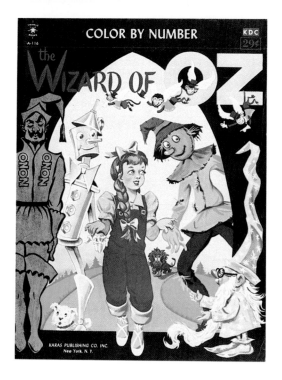

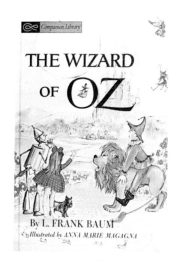

Another *Wizard of Oz* picturebook adaptation that enjoyed publishing longevity was Grossett & Dunlap's 1962 "Silver Dollar Edition," so named because of its original one dollar retail price.

Lowe's *Wizard of Oz Coloring Book*, circa the early 1960s, followed, in brief, the original L. Frank Baum story.

The Karas Publishing Company issued its Oz coloring book in 1962 as one of a series of color-by-number "Twinkle Books." This edition was also sold in the early 1980s with a slightly revised cover.

An unabridged version of *The Wizard of Oz* appeared in 1963 as part of Grossett & Dunlap's Companion Library. It was also available in a different jacket design as a Texaco gas station premium in addition to being bound as a single volume with Kipling's *The Jungle Book*.

The liberally adapted play script for the Proctor & Gamble *Wizard of Oz* puppets (1965-69) featured one of W.W. Denslow's illustrations on the cover and further suggested that youngsters improvise their own scenarios using the Oz characters.

In 1967, Curtis Candy offered three "Off to See the Wizard" coloring books as premiums inside boxes of candy.

Hallmark published a softcover edition of *The Wizard of Oz* in 1966 as an oversized greeting card containing an adaptation of the familiar story along with three pop-up illustrations. *Courtesy Cathi Dentler.*

Random House included a *Wizard of Oz Pop-Up Book* as one in a series of classic tales ingeniously engineered in animated format. This toy/book combination recreated several memorable episodes from Baum's story in three-dimensional pop-up illustrations. It originally retailed for $2.95 in 1968 and was available in two different sizes.

Wizard of Oz Christmas Book was distributed by Gimbels' New York department stores for the 1968 holiday season.

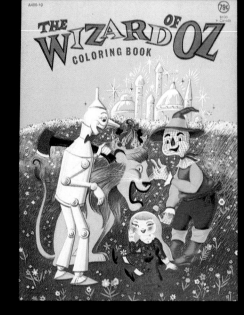

In 1969, Chicago's Children's Press published an oversized edition of *The Wizard of Oz* which contained a biography of L. Frank Baum and information about gemstones (left). The book was reprinted in 1970 by Modern Promotions and featured a new cover design (right).

An early-1970s *Wizard of Oz Coloring Book* was published by Playmore and reissued in 1984. This version of the oft-told tale boasted a Dorothy attired in go-go boots throughout.

The Wonderful Wizard of Oz Coloring Book (1974, Dover) contained an abridged text and dozens of black-and-white illustrations derived from the original book. Strong supporters of children's literature classics, Dover Publishing was also responsible for several Oz-inspired novelty books including *Wizard of Oz Stickers and Seals* and *Wizard of Oz Postcards*. In addition, the publisher reprinted Baum's first four Oz books in softcover volumes.

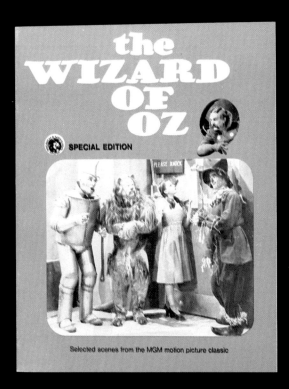

Selected scenes from the MGM motion picture classic

MGM Merchandising, in association with the Singer Sewing Machine Company, printed a *Wizard of Oz* "special edition" picture booklet to tie in with the 1970 television broadcast of the film. The booklet featured twenty-two pages of sequentially arranged photographs from the "MGM motion picture classic."

Well over twenty years after the Little Golden Book Oz story adaptations appeared, Western Publishing printed an edition of *The Wizard* that retained elements of Baum's story, but whose characters were definitely MGM-inspired.

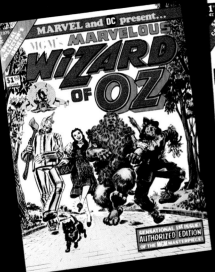

In connection with their Little Golden Book edition of *The Wizard of Oz*, Western Publishing issued a vastly abridged version of the story as one of the Golden Shape Book Series (1975).

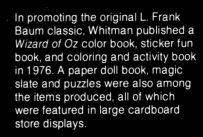

In promoting the original L. Frank Baum classic, Whitman published a *Wizard of Oz* color book, sticker fun book, and coloring and activity book in 1976. A paper doll book, magic slate and puzzles were also among the items produced, all of which were featured in large cardboard store displays.

Enthusiastic comic book adaptations of MGM's *The Wizard of Oz* (left) and Baum's *The Land of Oz* (right) both appeared in 1975 through the efforts of Marvel and DC Comics. Due to an agreement with MGM, the characters in both stories were required to resemble the movie conceptions—an idea that clashed with Marvel's *Land of Oz* artwork which was strongly reminiscent of John R. Neill's original illustrations. Unfortunately for fans, a proposed third book in the series, *Ozma of Oz*, was never realized.

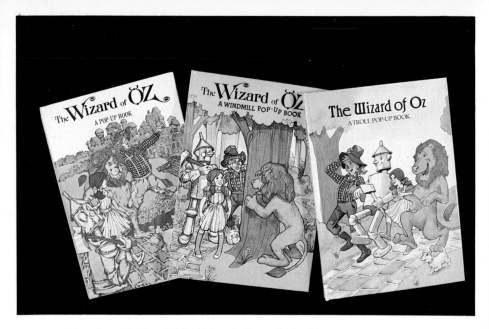

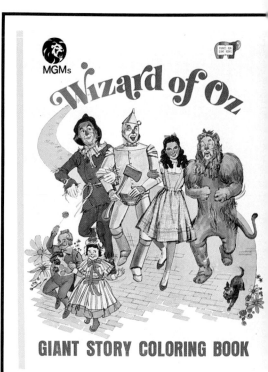

GIANT STORY COLORING BOOK

Price, Stern & Sloan's *The Wizard of Oz Pop-Up Book* (left) was first published in 1976, however a 1982-83 Windmill edition utilized the exact art and paper mechanics albeit with a new cover design (center). A more recent version with yet another cover was published by Troll Books (right).

This MGM *Wizard of Oz Giant Story Coloring Book* measured an oversized 17" x 22" and was published in 1976 by the Parkes Run Publishing Company. The cover was derived from the 1972 reissue theater poster artwork while the book's thirty-two pages to color were based upon drawings contained within the 1975 Marvel/DC comic book. In 1981 and 1984, Stoneway Ltd. reprinted this same book with a new cover.

In 1976, both Grossett & Dunlap (left) and Harper & Row (right) published softcover "movie editions" of *The Wizard of Oz* profusely illustrated with black-and-white frame blowups of film scenes throughout. The Grossett & Dunlap book was also printed as a hardbound edition.

Hallmark's *The Wizard of Oz* was one in a series of quality pop-up books published by the greeting card company circa 1977. The book recounted Baum's original plot through moveable and three-dimensional pictures. *Courtesy Cathi Dentler.*

Judy Garland in The Wizard of Oz was one in a number of "Magic Punch-Out See-Thru" novelty storybooks published in 1977 by Ottenheimer and distributed by Sharon Marketing. Despite plot liberties that varied from the film on which it was based, the book's illustrations captured the likenesses of the actors in character.

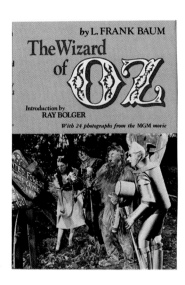

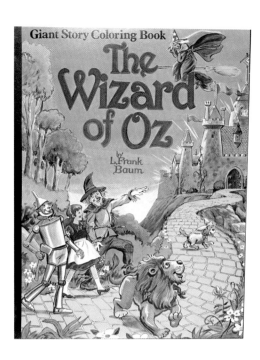

A Giant Story Coloring Book version of *The Wizard of Oz* with illustrations heavily inspired by the 1944 Evelyn Copelman edition was printed in 1980 by Colorful Fundraising, Inc. Inserted into each book was a T-shirt iron-on transfer, the picture of which was derived from the cover art of a similar coloring book.

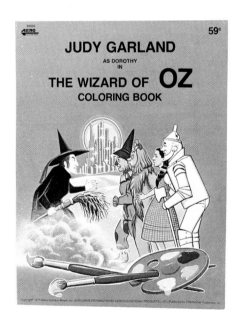

With an introduction by actor Ray Bolger, this hardcover edition of *The Wizard of Oz* featured twenty-four MGM movie stills on sixteen of its pages and was published as a special Doubleday Book Club selection in 1978.

Also in 1977, Ottenheimer printed a *Judy Garland as Dorothy in The Wizard of Oz Coloring Book*, distributed by Aero Educational Products, Ltd.

Dover Publishing printed two ingenious activity books designed by Oz and Baum historian/illustrator Dick Martin: *Cut and Assemble the Emerald City of Oz* (1980) and *Cut and Assemble the Wizard of Oz Toy Theater* (1985).

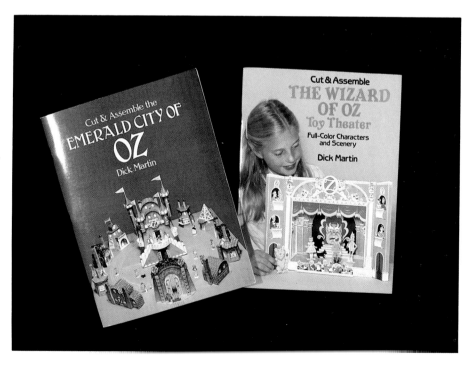

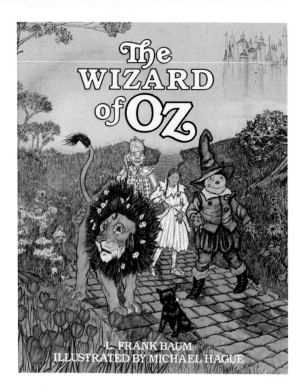

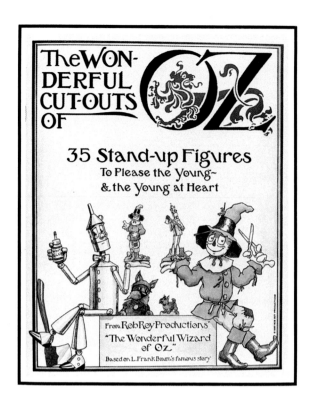

Hailed as a modern day Maxfield Parrish, children's book illustrator Michael Hague presented his vision of Oz in a 1982 edition of the L. Frank Baum story published by Holt, Rinehart and Winston. To promote the book, a full-color poster reproduction of the cover artwork was distributed.

Published in 1985 by Crown, *The Wonderful Cut-Outs of Oz* included all of the famous characters as drawn by Rob Roy Productions' studio in connection with their on-going animated adaptation of the original L. Frank Baum tale.

To take advantage of pre-publicity surrounding the summer, 1985 release of Disney's *Return to Oz*, Del-Rey Books promoted its series of paperback printings of many of the Oz books through colorful counter displays and heralds.

A 1985 adaptation of *The Wizard of Oz* was one in a series of lavishly illustrated classic novels published by Unicorn Books (left). In it, fantasy illustrator Greg Hildebrandt interpreted the beloved tale with vivid paintings that glowed with a life of their own. An abridged edition was published in 1988 (right) and in the intermittent years the book's paintings inspired a coloring book, a puzzle and a thirty-five panel fold-out frieze.

A novelization of the *Return to Oz* screenplay was published in paperback format by Del-Rey Books in 1985. Meshing elements from Baum's *The Land of Oz* and *Ozma of Oz*, it was written by Joan Vinge, author of the best-selling *Return of the Jedi* novelization, and featured eight pages of color stills.

Scholastic published a full-color comic book adaptation of *Return to Oz* in 1985.

Western Publishing's 1985 Little Golden Books and Golden Look-Look Books series included four *Return to Oz* titles which collectively recounted the movie's story through photographs and illustrations.

In 1985, Random House published *Walt Disney Pictures Presents Return to Oz* as one of its "Disney's Wonderful World of Reading" titles. Adapted from the film for very young readers, the picturebook was illustrated with color photographs.

Four different *Return to Oz* activity books based on the Walt Disney Pictures film were issued by Western Publishing in 1985.

One of many publications issued to take advantage of the *Return to Oz* publicity in 1985 was *The Wizard of Oz, A Story to Color* by Random House (left). Packaged with crayons and an audio cassette, it was reprinted by Warren, a Random House division, in 1987 (right).

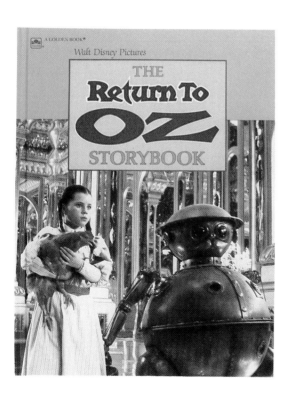

The Return to Oz Storybook, printed by Western Publishing in 1985, was lavishly pictured with color frame enlargements from the Disney film.

The Oz/Wonderland Wars (1986, DC Comics) documented the skirmish resulting when Baum and Neill's Oz characters clashed with Lewis Carroll and John Tenniel's literary figures. The saga "starring" Captain Carrot and his Amazing Zoo Crew unfolded in three issues overseen by Roy Thomas, who had scripted and edited the 1975 DC and Marvel Oz comic books.

The Spanish release of Cinar Films' 1987 animated production of *The Wonderful Wizard of Oz* prompted a sticker book (left) and comic book (right) as tie-ins in 1988. *Courtesy Tod Machin; photo: JoAnn Groves.*

A thirty-two page *Wizard of Oz Coloring Book* was one of many souvenirs sold at performances of *The Wizard of Oz Live!* in 1989. The book's settings were all patterned after those in the arena tour production. *Courtesy Tricia Trozzi.*

This 1988 "Sticker Fun" book by Western Publishing contained twenty different MGM movie scene stickers to be mounted and cut out as trading cards.

The Wizard of Oz Big Color/Activity Book featured pictures to color based on frames taken directly from the MGM film as well as other Ozzy puzzles and activities. Published in 1988, the book was available in retail stores in addition to being offered as a premium for Dixie's Oz kitchen cups the following year.

Published in 1989 by Western Publishing Company, *The Wizard of Oz Movie Storybook* by Jan Wahl gave a brief retelling of the story "illustrated with full-color stills from the original movie!" The book initially retailed for $6.95.

Effectively fusing L. Frank Baum's fantasy with realism, Charles Santore's paintings for this 1991 edition of *The Wizard of Oz* (Jellybean Press) have been unanimously proclaimed one of the most beautiful artist interpretations of all time.

Buttons, Badges and Pins

Two variants of a promotional "What Did the Woggle Bug Say?" celluloid pin-back button were distributed to patrons by newspapers carrying Baum's "Queer Visitors From the Marvelous Land of Oz" comic page in 1904-05. (A contemporary *Publisher's Weekly* advertisement announced that five hundred thousand such buttons would be distributed.) The catch phrase was initiated in connection with a contest whereby clever readers guessed the Woggle Bug's riddle inherent in the comic's text. Some newspapers printed their titles along the rim edge of the buttons they gave out.

To advertise the 1915 publication of *The Scarecrow of Oz*, Reilly & Britton commissioned the Parisian Novelty Company in Chicago to manufacture celluloid buttons depicting the book's title character. *Courtesy the Baum Collection, Alexander Mitchell Library.*

In the weeks prior to the August, 1939 release of MGM's *The Wizard of Oz*, theater ushers wore promotional "Coming Soon!" buttons manufactured by the Economy Novelty & Printing Company. *Courtesy Michael Patrick Hearn; photo: David Moyer.*

"The Wizard is Coming" announced a rayon advertising tag made by Whitney Manufacturing for wear by theater employees prior to the release of the MGM movie in 1939. *Courtesy Meinhardt Raabe.*

To promote the 1939 film, sets of five *Wizard of Oz* pin-back buttons were made by the Economy Novelty & Printing Company in New York. According to the movie campaign book, theater owners were encouraged to distribute the 1¼-inch buttons for contest purposes, identifying winners by the numbers printed on each. Identical ⅞-inch versions were also manufactured in late 1939 for the Mexican release of the movie. Such examples were marked either *El Mago de Oz* or *El Brujo de Oz*, however none featured the contest numbers found on the American buttons. *Judy Garland button courtesy Hake's Americana & Collectibles, York, PA; photo: Russ King.*

In 1939, the Loew's theater chain advertised the product of its studio affiliate through *Wizard of Oz* buttons illustrated with Al Hirschfeld's Scarecrow caricature. *Courtesy Hake's Americana & Collectibles, York, PA.*

In 1967, Samson Products made a set of twelve ⅞-inch "Off to See the Wizard" pin-back buttons for bubblegum machine sale.

Costume jewelry pins of at least the Scarecrow and Tin Man were marketed in 1939 by the Hollywood Jewelry Company. *Courtesy Larry Schlick.*

At least three "Land of Oz" pin-back buttons were available at the North Carolina theme park during the 1970s. *Courtesy Hake's Americana & Collectibles, York, PA; photo: Russ King.*

71

"Emerald City Police" badges and pins were bestowed to fans dedicated to upholding the Law of Oz in the early 1980s. *Courtesy Tod Machin; photo: JoAnn Groves.*

At least eight different 1¾-inch pin-back buttons produced by Button-Up Company circa 1986 combined the classic MGM Oz movie characters with contemporary humor and catch phrases of the day. A number of similar keychains were also marketed.

This 1¼-inch *Return to Oz* pre-production pin-back button was distributed by the Disney Studios in 1984 to promote its forthcoming motion picture, simply titled *Oz* at the time.

In promotion of its month-long *Wizard of Oz* fiftieth anniversary celebration during the summer of 1989, Macy's department stores provided employees with 3-inch buttons to be worn as advertisement. Both the artwork appearing on the button and the slogan "It's Oz Time at Macy's" were used extensively for poster, flyer and newspaper publicity. *Courtesy Tod Machin; photo: JoAnn Groves.*

Not intended for retail sale, these 1⅛-inch commemorative cloisonne pins were handed out as promotional items during press conferences and other publicity generating events for MGM/UA's Fiftieth Anniversary Edition *Wizard of Oz* video release.

A sparkling ruby slippers pin commemorated the 1939 film's fiftieth anniversary and was sold at performances of *The Wizard of Oz Live!. Courtesy Chris Sterling.*

Gold and silver plated costume jewelry pins based on the MGM Oz movie characters were manufactured by Wendy Gell Jewelry of New York. These and a host of similar pins adorned with crystals, pave, rhinestones and such were made available by the company in honor of *The Wizard*'s fiftieth anniversary in 1989.

Employees of Whataburger restaurants of Arizona, Tennessee, Oklahoma, Texas and Florida donned several different 3-inch crew buttons as advertisement for the company's *Wizard of Oz* fiftieth anniversary drinking glass promotion in 1989. In addition to the six buttons shown here, there was also another button featuring the Wicked Witch of the West with her famous line, "I'll get you my pretty!" *Courtesy Tod Machin; photo: JoAnn Groves.*

This 3¼-inch button proclaimed, "I saw *The Wizard of Oz* World Arena Tour" (1989). *Courtesy Chris Sterling.*

Pfizer Laboratories promoted arthritis awareness through a 1989 campaign featuring an MGM Tin Man look-alike on pin-back buttons. *Courtesy Michael Patrick Hearn; photo: David Moyer.*

Collector's Items

An early-1970s mail-order catalogue offering included this hand-painted porcelain music box which was marked only "Japan." Though the adorning figures were clearly book-inspired, the music played "Over the Rainbow" when the circular base was wound. *Courtesy Bill Beem.*

A musical Dorothy and Toto figurine was made in Japan and distributed by Spencer Gifts in 1974. When wound it played "Over the Rainbow." *Courtesy Tod Machin; photo: JoAnn Groves.*

"Over the Rainbow," Copyright
1977 MGM.

"If I Were King of the Forest,"
Copyright 1978 MGM.

"If I Only Had a Brain," Copyright
1977 MGM.

"If I Only Had a Heart," Copyright
1978 MGM.

"Wicked Witch of the West,"
Copyright 1979 MGM.

"Follow the Yellow Brick Road,"
Copyright 1979 MGM.

"Wonderful Wizard of Oz,"
Copyright 1979 MGM.

Two different sets of *Wizard of Oz*
wooden Christmas ornaments were
manufactured by Kurt S. Adler, Inc.
The figures along the bottom were
from an early-1980s set that
included the good and wicked
witches. The set above those was
marked "1984" and included jointed
"jumping jack" figures.
Accompanying the latter set was a
tiny edition of *The Wizard* which
featured a condensed (though
faithful) text and a number of
illustrations reproduced from W.W.
Denslow's original artwork.

° "The Grand Finale (We're Off to
See the Wizard)," Copyright 1979
MGM.

Artist James A. Auckland had the
distinction of painting the first series
of collector plates ever produced to
commemorate a motion picture and
The Wizard of Oz became the film
so honored. The limited edition
plates were issued by the Edwin M.
Knowles China Company from 1977
to 1979 and were extremely popular
among Oz collectors and plate
enthusiasts alike. (Beginning in
1991, Knowles introduced a second
series of MGM Oz plates

These attractive figural music
boxes were patterned after the
MGM movie characters and
produced by Schmid in 1983.
Although the Dorothy music box
played "Over the Rainbow," the

In 1988, The Hamilton Collection introduced *The Wizard of Oz Commemorative Plate Collection* to honor the approaching fiftieth anniversary of the MGM motion picture classic. Each of the eight fine porcelain collector plates in the series depicted a memorable scene from *The Wizard* as created by cinematic art master Thomas Blackshear and was rimmed with a 23K gold "yellow brick road" border. The 8½-inch plates were limited to an edition of fourteen firing days and were accompanied by an individually numbered certificate of authenticity.

"The Tin Man Speaks"

"We're Off to See the Wizard"

"Dorothy Meets the Scarecrow"

"A Glimpse of the Munchkins"

"The Witch Casts a Spell"

"The Great and Powerful Oz"

"If I Were King of the Forest"

"There's No Place Like Home"

Several sizes of collector Christmas ornaments were made by Kurt S. Adler, Inc. and distributed by Santa's World for the 1987 holiday season. Also at that time, the company marketed a set of four 24-inch motorized Oz statuettes, Ozzy cloth Christmas bags, tree skirts, paper garland, music boxes and snow domes—all modeled in comparable character likenesses. *Courtesy Chris Sterling.*

The Hamilton Collection's series of porcelain *Wizard of Oz* bells was introduced in 1988. Each of the twelve pieces in the series stood approximately 5 inches high and featured a charming portrayal of one of the memorable Oz film characters perched atop an octagonal bell ornamented with a shining 24K gold band and "Oz" inscription. A separate, similar bell was also manufactured featuring the famous ruby slippers in place of a character as was a tiny "ruby slipper" bell-shaped thimble.

Enesco's elaborate Oz musical jack-in-the-boxes were produced as a "limited edition" of seventy-five hundred sets in order to commemorate the fiftieth anniversary of the MGM motion picture. The four principal characters were introduced in 1988 while "Glinda" and "The Wicked Witch of the West" were marketed a year later as was a smaller set of all six which not only played music from the film's songs (as the larger ones did), but also became "animated" when wound.

Seven different wooden musical jewelry boxes were issued by Presents of California in 1988 and 1989, as was a porcelain ruby slippers trinket box. Each of the "limited edition" music boxes played one of the memorable tunes from the MGM motion picture and was accompanied by a hand-numbered certificate of authenticity. *Courtesy Presents of California.*

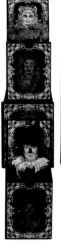

The Caribbean island of Montserrat (through D & G Philatelic of West Hempstead, New York) issued a set of four stamps and a souvenir sheet in 1989 to commemorate the fiftieth anniversary of MGM's *The Wizard of Oz*. A special first day cover envelope was issued in conjunction with the stamps as well.

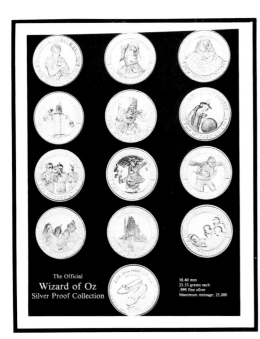

The Official Wizard of Oz Silver Proof Collection was a set of twelve proofs of .999 fine silver measuring 38.40mm in diameter and featuring character likenesses and other images from the beloved MGM movie. Issued as fiftieth anniversary commemoratives, each of the twenty-five thousand finely crafted sets came replete with its own custom display case, a certificate of authenticity, and a special thirty-six-page *Wizard of Oz* booklet. The company concurrently issued ten thousand similar sets of .999 *gold* proofs consisting of six pieces which measured 20mm in diameter. *Courtesy Paramount International Coin Corporation.*

This "Fifty Years of Oz" porcelain collector plate offered a striking montage tribute to the 1939 film by artist Thomas Blackshear framed with an 8mm decorative border of 23K gold. Issued by The Hamilton Collection in cooperation with MGM and Turner Entertainment as the "official commemorative collector plate for the Golden Anniversary of *The Wizard of Oz*," the plate measured an oversized 9¼ inches in diameter and was voted 1990 "Plate of the Year" by the National Association of Limited Edition Dealers.

The Enesco Treasury of Christmas Ornaments included a set of four *Wizard of Oz* pieces which were hand-painted and crafted from a moldable material called Artplas. Marketed as "limited edition" fiftieth anniversary collectibles, the ornaments were produced for 1989 only.

Also available from Enesco in 1989 was "The Yellow Brick Road" revolving musical which featured all of the Oz travelers and played "We're Off to See the Wizard" when switched on.

Part of Enesco's *Wizard of Oz Fiftieth Anniversary Collection* was a set of four revolving musicals representing the famous MGM film personalities. Licensed by Turner Entertainment Company in 1988 (but not marketed until 1989), each of the characters played a different tune from the movie's familiar score: Dorothy/"Over the Rainbow"; Scarecrow/"If I Only Had a Brain"; Tin Man/"We're Off to See the Wizard"; Cowardly Lion/"If I Were King of the Forest."

The Wizard of Oz Christmas Ornaments were officially authorized by Turner Entertainment prior to the 1989 holiday season. Each ornament in the set of twelve displayed a color scene from the 1939 movie framed with its own unique filigreed border design finished with 2.5 micro-inches of 24K gold. The ornaments came complete with a specially designed storage box and were available exclusively from The Danbury Mint of Norwalk, Connecticut. *Courtesy The Danbury Mint.*

The *Portraits From Oz Plate Collection* was a second series of eight fine porcelain collector plates produced by The Hamilton Collection in celebration of the fiftieth anniversary of *The Wizard of Oz*. Introduced in 1989, the 8½-inch plates in the collection once again offered the artwork of Thomas Blackshear, a "yellow brick road" border design of 23K gold, and an edition limited to a total of fourteen firing days.

"Tin Man"

"Dorothy"

"Cowardly Lion"

"Scarecrow"

Glinda

Wicked Witch of the West

Wizard

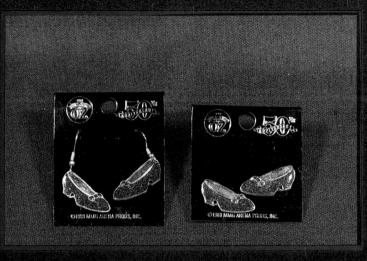

Two similar sets of earrings
depicting the famous ruby slippers
were sold throughout the 1989
national Wizard of Oz Live! tour.
Courtesy Chris Sterling

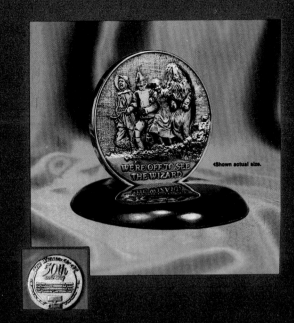

◀Shown actual size.

To honor The Wizard of Oz on its
golden anniversary, Creative
Minting, Inc. issued in a 3-inch Oz
medallion of gold-plated jewelers
pewter along with a custom
Venetian marble display base. One
side of the medallion bore the
likenesses of the film characters as
sculpted by award-winning artist
Sue Etem while the reverse was
inscribed with the character and
actor name for the famous
foursome. Limited to an edition of
twenty-five thousand, each
medallion carried its own serial
number and was accompanied by a
matching numbered certificate of
authenticity and a gift box. The
company also issued a similar
smaller medallion likewise cast in
pewter, but without the gold finish.
Courtesy Creative Minting, Inc.

The Franklin Mint produced this
Fiftieth Anniversary edition Wizard
of Oz chess set by the late 1989.
Designed by artist Isabella
Mazzanti, each of the thirty-two
of which pieces was cast in solid
American pewter and hand-painted
to represent one of the film's
characters. Also included as part of

the set was a playing board made
of assorted hardwoods. Note how
the creators have cleverly assumed
that various chess roles: the Lion as
King, Dorothy as Queen, the
Scarecrow as Bishop, the Tin Man
as Knight, the Emerald City as
Rook, and the Lollipop Guild as
Pawns.

For Christmas 1989, Presents of California adapted the heads of its fiftieth anniversary *Wizard of Oz* dolls for a set of six vinyl-and-cloth holiday ornaments. *Courtesy Presents of California.*

Presents also adapted its PVC figurines to produce six revolving Oz musicals in 1989. Dorothy and Glinda played "Over the Rainbow"; the Tin Man, Cowardly Lion and Wicked Witch played "We're Off to See the Wizard"; and the Scarecrow played "If I Only Had a Brain."

Artist Barry Leighton-Jones captured various MGM *Oz* scenes and characters in this colorful print distributed by Stanton Arts in 1989. Each print was signed, matted and displayed under glass with a 13½" x 11¾" gold frame. The same montage artwork was also available as a numbered, limited edition signed lithograph measuring 16" x 20".

The Hamilton Collection adapted four scenes from its *Wizard of Oz* commemorative plate collection to produce a set of diminutive porcelain trinket boxes in 1990. Distributed through the company's Presents of California division, all four boxes were available as both musical and non-musical variations.

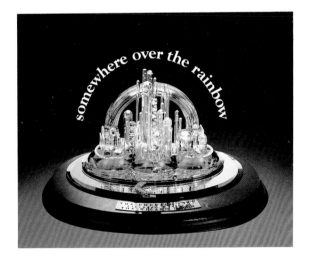

In 1990, designer Charles Castelli created a 5" x 8" Austrian crystal sculpture of the famous Emerald City. The piece was advertised as an official licensed edition and was available from the Crystallite Company, distributors and manufacturers of fine giftware and collectibles. *Courtesy Crystallite.*

The U.S. Postal Service issued a set of Classic Films Commemorative Stamps honoring the fiftieth anniversary of four Academy Award nominated motion pictures from 1939. Among the movies recognized on each of the twenty-five cent stamps were *Gone With the Wind*, *Beau Geste*, *Stagecoach* —and of course *The Wizard of Oz*. Touted as resembling miniature movie posters, the stamps were designed by artist Thomas Blackshear who likewise was responsible for the images appearing on The Hamilton Collection's fiftieth anniversary Oz collector plate series. The stamps were officially dedicated in Hollywood on March 23, 1990 as a prelude to the 62nd Annual Academy Awards held on March 26.

The Franklin Mint produced a series of *Wizard of Oz* musical sculptures that stood approximately 6½ inches high. Each of the intricately detailed, hand-painted porcelain scene sculptures was covered by a glass bell jar and mounted upon a wooden musical base which, when wound, played that particular tune for which the sculpture was named.

"If I Were King of the Forest" (1991). *Courtesy The Franklin Mint.*

"We're Off to See the Wizard" (1989). *Courtesy The Franklin Mint.*

"Follow the Yellow Brick Road" (1991). *Courtesy The Franklin Mint.*

Costumes and Masks

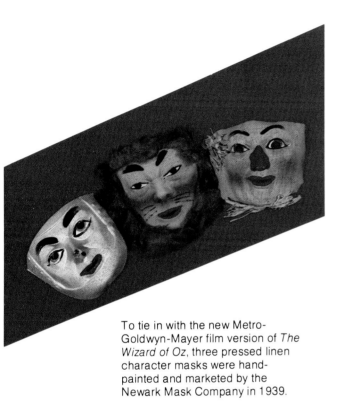

To tie in with the new Metro-Goldwyn-Mayer film version of *The Wizard of Oz*, three pressed linen character masks were hand-painted and marketed by the Newark Mask Company in 1939.

In September 1939, the Einson-Freeman Company issued this set of five paper character masks accompanied by a handout flyer entitled "Eight Ways to Have Fun at a Hallowe'en Party With Wizard of Oz Masks." Although similar masks of Glinda, the Wicked Witch and Nikko (the Witch's monkey servant) are rumored to exist, they were most likely to have been used only for display or promotion. The following November, the Santa Claus in the toy department of John Wanamaker's New York store handed out free Oz masks to young visitors.

Wizard of Oz's Wizard of Oz was one of the Halpern Company's Halco "superior brand" masquerade costume and mask sets in the 1961 "Tales of the Wizard of Oz" line. *Courtesy Cathi Dentler.*

Wizard of Oz's Rusty the Tin Man Masquerade Costume was also marketed by Halco in 1961 to tie in with the "Tales of the Wizard of Oz" cartoon program. In addition to its "Wizard," the same company issued at least one other Halloween costume of the show's "Dandy Lion" character.

The long-time Halloween costume company, Ben Cooper, introduced the "Off to See the Wizard" Scarecrow in 1967 followed by the Tin Man in 1968. The Scarecrow costume was one in the "Flick & Trick Lite-Up Mask" series and included a manually operated battery pack wired to a miniature light bulb centered on the mask. The Tin Man was marketed as late as 1973, as was a variant of the Scarecrow mask, sold separately from any outfit.

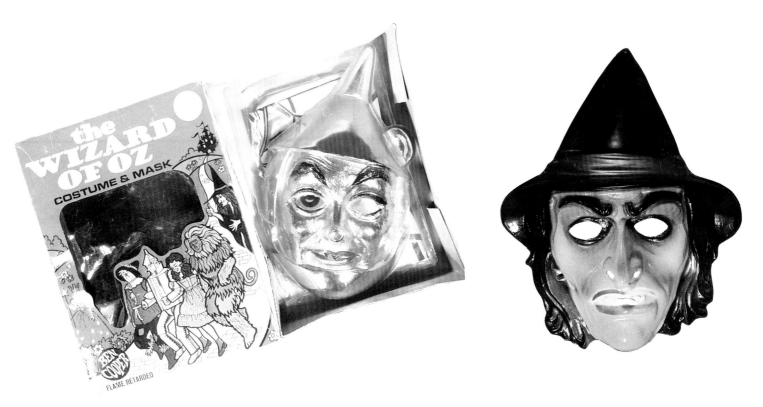

For Halloween 1975, Ben Cooper offered a set of Oz costumes which included at least Dorothy, Tin Woodman, and Cowardly Lion kits in addition to a separately sold Wicked Witch mask. The boxed costumes generally retailed for four dollars and the masks were usually marked with an official *Wizard of Oz* tag.

In 1982, Dover published Dick Martin's *Cut and Make Wizard of Oz Masks* containing eight color characters as inspired by *The Wonderful Wizard of Oz*. Courtesy Cathi Dentler.

McCall's offered these *Wizard of Oz* movie-based costume patterns in 1985. They were licensed by "MGM UA Entertainment Company."

Having originally issued a ceramic mask depicting Judy Garland as Dorothy circa 1986 among the various celebrity likenesses it produced, Clay Art company chose to manufacture similar masks of the three male Oz characters in 1989 in addition to a slightly revised version of Dorothy. Each of the four masks were available individually gift-boxed.

Don Post Studios, Inc. produced three rubber head masks of the Oz characters in 1983.

Each of Collegeville's four *Wizard of Oz* kiddie costumes consisted of the traditional plastic face mask and vinyl body suit. Although initially marketed in fall of 1989, the costumes were still available in some areas for Halloween of 1991.

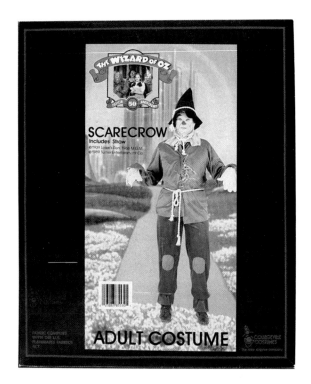

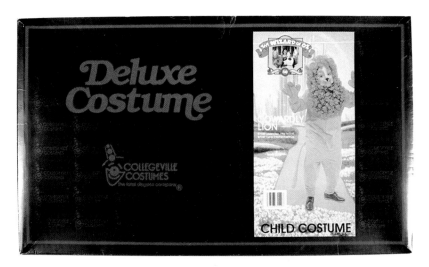

Collegeville Costumes also offered four different "deluxe" *Wizard of Oz* costumes in 1989, all of which came in both child and adult sizes.

Creative interpretations of the original Oz book characters were the basis for the four heavy paper masks included in this 1990 booklet printed by Watermill Press. *Courtesy Jane Albright; photo: JoAnn Groves.*

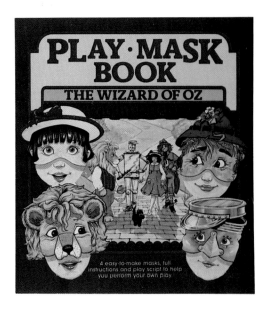

Dolls and Playsets

Four "cuddly toys to delight the heart of every youngster" were produced out of Frank J. Baum's Los Angeles based Oz Doll & Toy Manufacturing Company in 1924. Patterned after the celebrated book characters popularized by his father, L. Frank Baum, each 13-inch doll was based upon John R. Neill's illustrations and printed in color on

"art leather," then filled with kapok stuffing. Though the figures were charming, young Baum lacked the business expertise to effectively market them and he resorted to selling his remaining stock to Reilly & Lee, who then packaged the dolls in individually boxed sets, each with its own Oz book. Shown here are the Scarecrow, Jack Pumpkinhead

and the Patchwork Girl. (Not pictured is the Tin Woodman; refer to the advertisement on page 20) for an illustration.) *Patchwork Girl from private collection: Scarecrow and Jack Pumpkinhead courtesy Michael Patrick hearn; photos: David Moyer.*

"Judy Garland as Dorothy in *The Wizard of Oz*" was an all-composition doll manufactured by the Ideal Novelty & Toy Company in 1939. Garland's likeness was molded in 13-inch, 15½-inch, and 18-inch sizes by leading celebrity doll sculptor, Bernard Lipfert (the two largest dolls are shown). The doll wore a rayon jumper over an organdy blouse as adapted by Mary Bauer from Gilbert Adrian's original movie costume design. Inspired by the actress it portrayed, a unique feature of the Judy Garland doll was her overly large, expressive "open/close" brown eyes. Each doll was usually marked "Ideal Doll/Made in USA" at the base of the head, with "USA" and a number embossed on the back.

Also available from Ideal in 1939 was "The Strawman by Ray Bolger of *The Wizard of Oz*." This all-cloth doll was attired in a black or navy blue jacket and tan or pink trousers. It measured approximately 17 inches in height, although an unusual 21-inch version has surfaced in at least one instance as well. Upon seeing the doll many years later, Bolger himself remarked that it bore closer resemblance to Fred Stone, famed Scarecrow of the 1902 stage musical. Curiously, the doll's prototype was inspired by the traditional book character before its appearance was altered to better caricature Bolger in his movie role. This was perhaps due to a clause added to the actor's MGM contract stipulating that any imitation likeness of his character was required to include a tag stating that "...the Scarecrow in *The Wizard of Oz* was played by Ray Bolger."

The Artistic Toy Company introduced its "Tales of the Wizard of Oz" dolls at the 1962 New York Toy Fair trade show. Known examples of the 14-inch cloth-and-vinyl figures included "Dandy Lion," "Socrates, the Scarecrow" and "Rusty, the Tin Man." Each doll's head was marked "Artistic Toy" and "© Videocraft Ltd. 1962." *"Dandy Lion" doll courtesy of Rob Roy MacVeigh.*

This set of cloth *Wizard of Oz* dolls was a 1971 M-D Tissue premium. The series also included *Goldilocks and the Three Bears* and several *Alice in Wonderland* characters.

Though tagged "© 1967," Mattel made this "Off to See the Wizard" Scarecrow "Talkin' Patter Pillow" available for 1968 only. When his pull-string was drawn and released, the cloth-stuffed doll randomly repeated up to ten different sentences.

In 1975, the Mego Toy Corporation marketed a set of six 8-inch, authentically costumed vinyl *Wizard of Oz* dolls as inspired by the MGM movie favorite. The popular line underwent slight product and packaging revisions before being reissued later in the year. (Most significant of the changes was the fact that the Scarecrow was given "hair," presumably so little girls would have something to comb!) Anticipating that the Wicked Witch doll would be the least saleable in the set, it's interesting to note that Mego packed only one such doll per carton when shipping lots were sent to retail distributors.

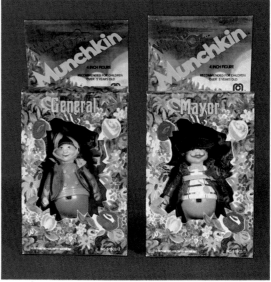

Marked "1974" but made available in 1975, Mego's *Wizard of Oz and His Emerald City Playset* was issued in conjunction with the six boxed character dolls made by the company the same year. The Wizard doll included in the set was also available separately from the playset in a plain brown shipping box exclusively through Sears. The set also contained a cardboard apple tree, a folding yellow brick road, a spinning crystal ball and the Wizard's throne.

To accompany the *Munchkinland Playset* in 1976, Mego made a set of 4-inch Munchkin citizen dolls. They included "Flower Girl," "Dancing Girl," "General" and "Mayor."

Due to the popularity of its *Wizard of Oz* doll line, Mego introduced a *Munchkinland Playset* in 1976, complete with a Munchkin Mayor doll, Dorothy's bed, and a "tornado transporter" that could carry Dorothy away from her Kansas bedroom to the magical Land of the Munchkins.

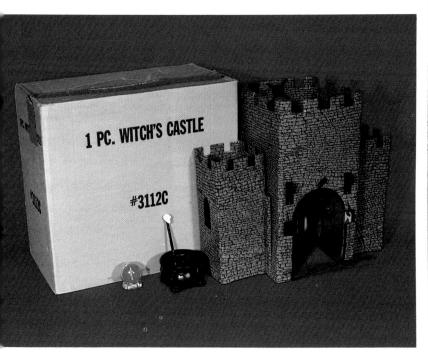

Available exclusively through Sears for Christmas 1975, Mego's *Witch's Castle Playset* came complete with the Wicked Witch doll, her cauldron, and a crystal ball. The green vinyl playset was merely sold in a plain brown shipping box.

The Toy Factory's *The Wonderful Wizard of Oz Paper Dolls* were intended to represent Baum's original story characters, though, perhaps in concession to film fans, Dorothy had a choice of either silver shoes or ruby slippers. The same company concurrently marketed a cardboard Emerald City playset in 1975.

These four oversized Mego dolls were reportedly made in only fifteen hundred sets during 1975 and test-marketed in select areas. Some of the dolls were also believed to have been warehoused and not "officially" distributed to the general public. Like their 8-inch counterparts, these 14-inch characters had well-sculpted heads but their bodies were cloth-stuffed.

This set of three cloth Oz dolls was originally offered in 1976 by the Jordan Marsh Company in sew-together kit form.

The Wizard of Oz Paper Dolls was printed in 1976 by Whitman Publishing as part of its line of activity books inspired by the famous story.

Wizard of Oz Doodle Dolls was a boxed kit marketed in 1979 by Crafts by Whiting, a division of Milton Bradley. Despite their rather generic appearance, the dolls were licensed by MGM. *Courtesy Cathi Dentler.*

The Wizard of Oz Doll Collection was introduced in 1982 exclusively through Dave Grossman Designs. Limited to 250 sets, each figure was sculpted and hand-painted in porcelain with glass eyes and was authentically costumed by noted artist Maureen Nalevanko from her Doll-Lain Studio. The dolls were permanently mounted on interconnecting yellow brick road bases and accompanied by certificates of authenticity. Since the set was licensed by MGM, Nalevanko required prior approval on each design. She had great difficulty receiving endorsement on her likeness of Judy Garland until her granddaughter single-handedly selected the prototype that best matched "Dorothy" from her favorite movie. The sculptress also marketed the dolls independently of Grossman Designs as the "Grand Finale," featuring all four characters joined arm-in-arm, attached to a wooden plaque base and limited to fifty sets. *Courtesy Dave Grossman Creations.*

Inspired by the popular reception of its Judy Garland as Dorothy doll a year earlier, Effanbee marketed this set of 11½-inch Oz dolls in 1985. In later years, the series was expanded to include the two witches, Auntie Em and Munchkins.

Akin to Effanbee's dolls, World Doll's "Wonderful Wizard of Oz Collection" was comprised of the same doll costumed differently for each individual character. The 8-inch dolls were fully jointed and each was accompanied by a certificate of authenticity. The Oz series was licensed by Turner Entertainment for a one-year production period beginning in 1987. *Courtesy World Doll.*

A highly successful set of *Wizard of Oz* vinyl dolls was produced by Presents of California, a division of Hamilton Gifts, Ltd. Dorothy, Scarecrow, Tin Man, and Lion were first introduced in 1988 as early fiftieth anniversary tie-ins. A year later Glinda and the Wicked Witch were added to the series, as well as a Lollipop Guild Boy, Lullabye League Girl and Mayor of Munchkinland. Also at this time, an improved likeness of Dorothy was issued. The dolls could be displayed on their specially designed yellow brick road doll stands and were widely available into 1990, at which time a Wizard doll was also manufactured.

101

Shortly after the 1982 production of her *Wizard of Oz* limited edition dolls, artist Maureen Nalevanko issued an expert likeness of Margaret Hamilton as the Wicked Witch of the West, sold in an edition of one hundred such examples. *Courtesy Maureen Nalevanko.*

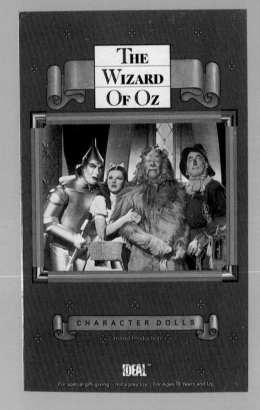

Left:
A 14½-inch "Judy Garland as Dorothy" doll was made in 1984 by Effanbee as sixth in the company's "Legend Series" line of authentically costumed vinyl dolls honoring famous personalities and celebrities. Among other "legends" portrayed in the series were W.C. Fields, John Wayne, Mae West, Groucho Marx, Louis Armstrong and Lucille Ball.

Right:
Ideal's 1984 *Wizard of Oz* "Character Dolls" stood approximately 9 inches high and came packaged in a storybook box decorated with a scene from the MGM movie. Promoted as "limited production" collectibles, the dolls were intended as gift-giving items (rather than play toys) "for ages twelve years and up."

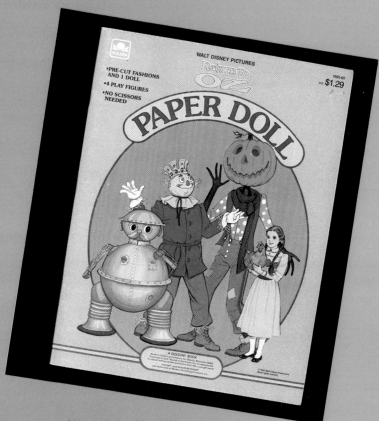

Although the title of Western Publishing's *Return to Oz Paper Doll Book* (1985) suggested an activity book limited to one punchout figure, stand-up dolls of the Scarecrow, Tik-Tok, and Jack Pumpkinhead were included along with several wardrobe changes for Dorothy.

Famous for its fine quality collector's items, The Franklin Mint introduced its elaborate porcelain-and-cloth "Judy Garland as Dorothy" doll as early as 1986 in anticipation of the fiftieth anniversary of MGM's *The Wizard of Oz*. In the years to follow, the company would produce an entire line of such dolls that included the Cowardly Lion (1987), the Tin Man (1988), the Scarecrow (1989), Glinda (1989), the Wicked Witch of the West (1990) and The Wizard (1991). A custom display "Emerald City of Oz" setting for the dolls was also made available in conjunction with the series in 1990.

"Bert Lahr as the Cowardly Lion," second in the series, stood approximately 21 inches tall. *Courtesy The Franklin Mint.*

"Ray Bolger as the Scarecrow," fourth in the series, stood approximately 22 inches tall. *Courtesy The Franklin Mint.*

"Judy Garland as Dorothy," first in The Franklin Mint's *Wizard of Oz* doll series, stood approximately 17 inches tall and held Toto in her real wicker basket. The doll here stands upon the company's "Emerald City of Oz" custom display which measured 12" deep x 32" wide x 25½" high. *Courtesy The Franklin Mint.*

"Jack Haley as the Tin Man," third in the series, stood approximately 22 inches tall. *Courtesy The Franklin Mint.*

"Margaret Hamilton as the Wicked Witch of the West," sixth in the series, stood approximately 21 inches tall. *Courtesy The Franklin Mint.*

"Billie Burke as Glinda," fifth in the series, stood approximately 19 inches tall. *Courtesy The Franklin Mint.*

"Toto too?"—Recreations of Dorothy's ever-popular dog (as portrayed by Terry the cairn terrier in the MGM movie) were marketed in the form of stuffed plush dolls and flocked vinyl figures by Presents of California beginning in 1988. *Courtesy Presents of California.*

"Frank Morgan as the Wizard of Oz," seventh in the series, stood approximately 19 inches tall. *Courtesy The Franklin Mint.*

These *Wizard of Oz* character dolls were among the earliest fiftieth anniversary tie-ins to hit the general public when they reached toy stores in 1988. The four principal characters and the two witches were sold both individually and in a "Collector's Edition" boxed set while the six "Munchkins" (including a winged monkey) were all sold separately. The Wizard doll was made available well over a year after the other dolls were first introduced.

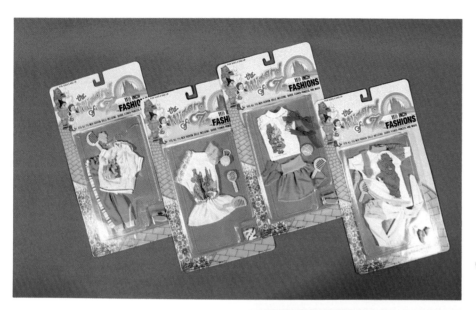

Aside from its own line of *Wizard of Oz* dolls in 1988, the Multi Toys Corporation marketed a variety of Oz-inspired clothing for other dolls ranging from Barbie doll-sized fashions to baby doll outfits to "dress-up costumes" of the actual Oz characters.

Cloth dolls of *The Wizard of Oz Live!* arena tour characters were made in at least three different sizes by Applause, Inc. and sold as souvenirs to attenders of the musical production. *Courtesy Chris Sterling.*

Largo Toys sold its charming set of four movie-based character rag dolls in 1989 as "The Original Soft Doll of Oz." The boxes recommended the dolls for those ages 1½ to 99!

In 1990, Multi Toys Corporation issued each of its previously successful *Wizard of Oz* poseable figures as part of six different "Storybook" playsets, each of which also included a Munchkin figure, a story, decorative labels and accessories.

"Dorothy" was among various
"Storyland Dolls" produced by the
Madame Alexander Doll Company
in 1991. In addition to this particular
8-inch doll, a similar yet larger
"Dorothy" wearing a solid blue
pinafore was manufactured by the
company a year earlier.

Domestics and Housewares

Bissell's 1939 New Wizard carpet sweeper was illustrated with character decals remarkably similar to the W.L. Stensgaard store display art. The sweeper was marketed as late as 1941.

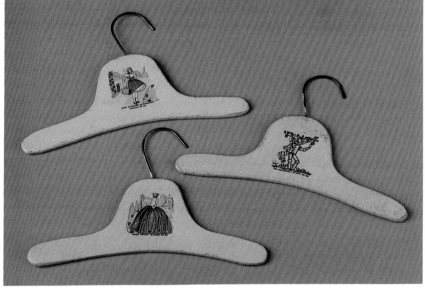

At least five different wooden clothes hangers with Oz character decals were produced in 1939 by Barney Stempler & Sons. Interestingly, the winged monkey, Nikko, was the only non-Baum character used in promoting the MGM film. Dorothy, Good Witch, and Tin Woodman hangers courtesy Tod Machin; photo: JoAnn Groves.

To tie in with the 1939 movie campaign, Brian Fabrics marketed *Wizard of Oz* rayon scarves which were printed in two different designs and a rainbow of color schemes. (A similar *Gone With the Wind* scarf was available in as many as ten different hues!) Curiously, the scarves were marked "Metro-Goldwyn-Mayer" instead of the customary "Loew's" copyright. *Variant scarf courtesy Hake's Americana & Collectibles, York, PA; photo: Russ King.*

New York's Herz & Kory Company marketed a child-sized "Judy Garland" handbag as part of the *Wizard of Oz* campaign in 1939. The alligator-textured patent leather purse contained a small fabric carrying case with mirror and was packaged in a plain box marked "Fine Arts Bags." The tag identified Garland as a "Metro-Goldwyn-Mayer Film Star," however the photo of the actress used was one of her earliest publicity portraits. *Courtesy Hake's Americana & Collectibles, York, PA.*

In the 1950s and 1960s, Swift & Company packaged their Oz Peanut Butter in 2½ and 5-pound tin pail containers. The red and yellow tins were most likely the earliest to be issued since the character designs closely resembled those used on the accompanying glass tumblers. The largest container in this style was also made with the word "sand" absent from the title printed around the can's rim.

A circa 1940 twelve-ounce "vacuum packed" metal container for Swift & Company's Oz-The Wonderful Peanut Spread. *Courtesy Bill Beem.*

Oz Fudge Mix was made by Homix Products, Inc. of New York circa late-1950s to early-1960s. *Courtesy Tod Machin; photo: JoAnn Groves.*

This circa late-1960s coaster tile derived its artwork from the cover of the 1950 Random House edition of *The Wizard of Oz*.

An Oz fabric pattern for curtains and bedspreads was produced circa the late-1950s or early-1960s by Home Fabrics and Draperies, Inc. *Courtesy Rob Roy MacVeigh.*

A circa 1962 Fieldcrest Line of *Wizard of Oz* "coordinated fashions for bed and bath" included blankets, pillow cases, sheets and towels. *Courtesy Tod Machin; photo: JoAnn Groves.*

An oversized *Wizard of Oz* pillow adapted its artwork from the film's 1972 theatrical reissue poster. It was distributed in the mid-1970s by Modern Pillow Company of New York. *Courtesy Bill Beem.*

"Ouchless" Curad Comic Strips Plastic Bandages were marketed by Kendall in 1968—promoting "Off to See the Wizard" and home health care!

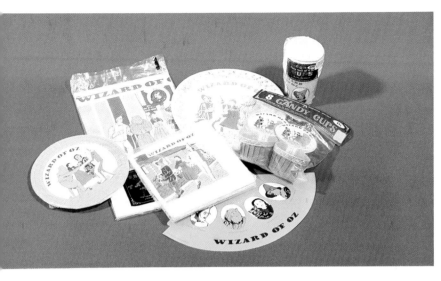

In 1975, Unique Industries issued a line of MGM *Wizard of Oz* paper party goods including hats, napkins, tablecloths, nut cups, drinking cups, and plates.

Scenes from MGM's *The Wizard of Oz* decorated a metal trash can produced in 1975 and marked "Cheinco Made in USA."

Hallmark offered an extensive line of Oz party goods circa 1975 which featured napkins, plates, and centerpieces in addition to a host of other accessories. At about this same time, American Greetings also sold Oz party items that included decorative wrapping paper.

Undoubtedly inspired by the Marvel/DC comic book art, an unidentified maker printed Oz wallpaper circa 1976.

In 1976, Perfect Fit Industries marketed a set of Oz character sheets and pillow cases illustrated with movie scenes taken from both the Marvel/DC comic book art and a contemporary wall poster designed by John Trull. The fabrics were marked only "© 1939 Ren. '66 MGM."

Bucilla marketed a 24″ x 28″ "Follow the Yellow Brick Road" Oz needle craft picture kit circa 1977 depicting the famous characters—once again patterned after the Marvel/DC comic book cover. The company also produced charming Oz needlepoint Christmas ornament kits about this same time as well. *Courtesy Jean Schreiner.*

A 3-foot by 5-foot *Land of Oz* baby quilt embroidery kit was available with matching bibs through *Family Circle* magazine in July 1977. *Courtesy Jean Schreiner.*

This Oz beach towel, circa 1976, unabashedly derived its artwork directly from the cover of the 1975 Marvel/DC comic book.

the **WIZARD of OZ** 1977

Printed in Romania and packaged in a decorative envelope, the Franco company marketed an Oz movie calendar towel for use in 1977.

The Original WIZARD of OZ **SCARECROW**

In 1984, Dalen Products, Inc. manufactured *The Original Wizard of Oz Scarecrow*, a 6-foot inflatable figure which could either be used for practical purposes or collected in its own right. Interestingly enough, the Scarecrow's clothing corresponds to that of his movie counterpart.

Indiana Metal Craft's Oz belt buckle (produced circa 1978) drew its engraved likeness from an Evelyn Copelman book painting. The reverse bore a brief passage from *The Wizard of Oz* that described the characters' first glimpse of the Emerald City. *Courtesy Rob Roy MacVeigh.*

A movie-influenced brass belt buckle was available only in Kansas in 1985, shortly after the state adopted its "Land of Ahs" slogan. The buckle was manufactured by Award Design Medals, Inc., an *Oklahoma* based company!

Landmark General Corporation printed *The Wizard of Oz Calendar* for the year 1985, incorporating twelve monthly frame blowups from the MGM movie classic. As an added bonus, an 8" x 10" "double laminated frameable print" was included. The calendar originally retailed for $8.95.

Five different Ozzy tins were produced by Presents of California in 1988, available with or without two sets of diminutive playing cards contained within.

In 1985, Jillson & Roberts produced a line of MGM-licensed gift wrappings which included decorative ribbon, two different styles of wrapping paper and a series of paper tote bags available in three sizes.

The Wizard of Oz was one of the many memorable films and famous personalities appearing on the faces of alarm clocks, pocket watches and other novelty timepieces manufactured by Westclock during the early 1980s.

Six figural *Wizard of Oz* magnets were licensed by MGM and manufactured by Grynnen Barrett in 1987.

Enesco's *Wizard of Oz* children's melamine dinnerware was marketed as a three-piece boxed set in 1989 to tie in with the movie's fiftieth anniversary.

The "50th Anniversary Commemorative Edition" *Wizard of Oz* 1989 calendar contained a short narrative regarding the making of the MGM motion picture in addition to twelve monthly frame blowups providing a brief chronology of the film's plot.

A plastic lunch kit sold by Aladdin Industries in 1989 featured a colorful decal decoration and a thermos with wraparound design.

A set of two free 11″ x 17″ *Wizard of Oz* placemats was offered by DowBrands during 1989 in exchange for two proofs-of-purchase from ZIPLOC Brand Storage, Freezer or Sandwich Bags, or tear strips from Handi-Wrap II or Saran Wrap.

MGM/UA Home Video produced beautifully embroidered jackets exclusively for use in promoting its Fiftieth Anniversary Edition *Wizard of Oz* videotape. The jackets were not available for purchase, but instead used as giveaways and prizes.

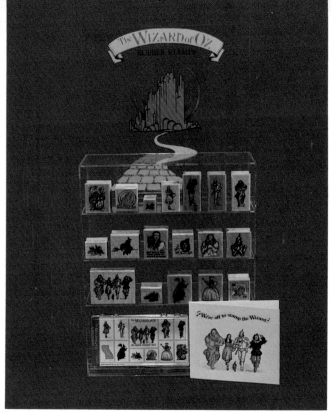

All Night Media's *Wizard of Oz* Collection offered an assortment of eighteen different wood-mounted rubber inking stamps representing characters and images from the 1939 film. Produced in 1989, the company also marketed eleven similar stamps as a set (bottom shelf) which included full-color indexing stickers and a 7″ x 3¾″ carrying case. The stamps here are shown perched upon a specially designed acrylic display made available to stores carrying the All Night Media Oz line.

Among the Ozzy goodies offered by Holiday Delites in 1989 were two-pound tins filled with character butter cookies (bottom right), Dorothy's Tin Basket featuring six ounces of hard candy (bottom left), a three-way popcorn assortment (top left) and twelve-ounce containers of Oz-shaped gummies (top right).

A 7-inch bone china "Scarecrow" nightlight was manufactured by Hamilton Gifts in 1989.

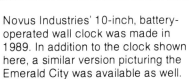

Novus Industries' 10-inch, battery-operated wall clock was made in 1989. In addition to the clock shown here, a similar version picturing the Emerald City was available as well.

Long-time "Dixie" cup manufacturer James River Corporation marketed its *Wizard of Oz* kitchen cups in 1989. Each of the seventeen different five-ounce cups featured surprisingly detailed drawings taken directly from MGM movie scenes. Also available was a complementing Oz cup dispenser, obtainable in retail stores or through a mail-order offer for $ 2.99.

Wendy Gell Jewelry, Inc. manufactured an extremely vivid cotton scarf licensed through Turner Entertainment for the fiftieth anniversary of *The Wizard of Oz* in 1989.

Paper Art Company's extensive line of Oz party goods included napkins, plates, table covers, hot/cold cups, invitations, centerpieces, hats, horns, flags, banners, loot bags, metallic balloons, door signs, and stickers (1989).

Applause's 1989 *Wizard of Oz* line included four different note pads, six figural erasers, four plastic message boxes, four different doorknob hangers, and various pens and pencils. *Courtesy Applause, Inc.*

120

Associated Marketing distributed its full-color *Wizard of Oz* "designer" pillow case in 1989.

Renaissance marketed a 30" x 60" *Wizard of Oz* beach towel in 1988 (left). Interestingly, the first towels manufactured credited Ray Bolger as the *Tin Man* and Jack Haley as the *Scarecrow* until being correctly revised the following year. In 1990 the company produced a second Oz towel (right)—this time with all cast members properly accounted for!

Clay Art issued two sets of licensed Oz salt and pepper shakers (one featuring Dorothy and friends, the other featuring the good and bad witches) as well as a complementing Emerald City napkin holder (1990).

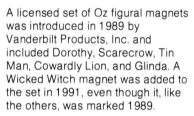

A licensed set of Oz figural magnets
was introduced in 1989 by
Vanderbilt Products, Inc. and
included Dorothy, Scarecrow, Tin
Man, Cowardly Lion, and Glinda. A
Wicked Witch magnet was added to
the set in 1991, even though it, like
the others, was marked 1989.

This Ozzy 1990 ceramic cookie jar
was hand-painted and made in the
Philippines by Clay Art.

Vanderbilt Products also
manufactured a variety of Wizard of
Oz stained-glass-like "suncatchers"
in 1989.

Figures and Figurines

Inspired by the MGM movie, Kerk Guild's *Soapy Characters From the Land of Oz* came packaged "For Fun in the Tub" and retailed for fifty cents in 1939. Each of the 4-inch figures in the set of five was hand-painted with varying degrees of effectiveness.

Hand-painted wood composition figures of the Scarecrow and Tin Woodman as they appeared in the MGM film were marked "Artisans Studio/Nashua N.H." and sold in 1939. The 4-inch high figures may have been unauthorized as they were not marked "Loew's Inc.", or they may have been manufactured by the official licensee, John C. Wellwood Corporation. *Courtesy Hake's Americana & Collectibles, York, PA.*

Hollow rubber figures of the Scarecrow, Tin Woodman, and Cowardly Lion were made by the A.A. Burnstein Sales Organization in 1939, and retailed for twenty-five cents each. According to press reports, the Tin Man was the first of the 7-inch characters to be produced—and was the only figure embossed with the actor's name and the movie title on his back. During the early 1940s, many patriotic children "did their part" for the war effort by donating such squeak toys to rubber recycling drives! *Scarecrow figure courtesy Hake's Americana & Collectibles, York, PA; photo: Russ King.*

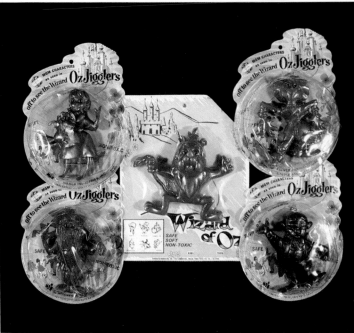

The Aurora Plastics Corporation, well-known model manufacturers, made a set of ten "Oz-Kins" available as a Burry Biscuit premium in 1967 (left). The set included an instruction leaflet, a paintbrush and paints. The same characters were later sold without accessories in a retail blister package (right) in promotion of ABC-TV's "Off to See the Wizard" cartoon program. The figures took their name from the Marx Company's popular plastic "Disneykins."

Six gelatin-like "Off to See the Wizard" *Oz Jigglers* were manufactured in early 1968 by Diener Industries and sealed on bubble pack display cards (left and right). The toys were later marketed by DMI Toys in an alternate packaging like that of the "Cowardly Lion" (center). *(Not pictured is the Tin Man; refer to the advertisement on page 31 for illustration).*

Multiple Toymakers marketed at least four "Rubb'r Niks" bendable figures of the "Off to See the Wizard" characters in 1967-68. Each was approximately 6 inches tall and originally sold sealed in a cardboard frame that cleverly incorporated the cartoon show's title while emphasizing *The Wizard of Oz*. Framed figures courtesy Chris Sterling.

Arnart Imports Incorporated marketed these unusual ceramic banks of the MGM characters circa the late 1960s. Each was identified with a paper tag listing the cast of film characters and packaged individually in a labeled box. The banks may have been sold as kits since they also have appeared in unpainted "greenware" form.

This strange 16-inch, carnival chalk Tin Man statuette was marked "1972" and "Tuscany Studios." A similar Scarecrow figure is known to exist, but may not have been made by the same manufacturer.

This set of four *Wizard of Oz* figurines was made circa the early 1970s by Pewter Fancy and sponsored by the New York Public Library. Each figure was patterned after the original book drawings by W.W. Denslow.

Four *Wizard of Oz* porcelain figurines produced by Seymour Mann were among the very first "quality" collectibles to be introduced. Sold in both toy stores and department stores in 1974, each figure originally carried a paper tag identifying the film actor and corresponding Oz character.

125

A pair of 15-inch ceramic figures of the Scarecrow and Tin Man were sold in craft shops during 1968 in both painted and unpainted form. *Courtesy Dede Schaeffer.*

This set of 6½-inch porcelain figurines was produced by Seymour Mann, Inc. and licensed by MGM. Although markings on the base of each figure identified them as being from 1981, they were widely available into 1985. The Mann company also marketed similar figurines as music boxes, in addition to a set of figurines depicting Dorothy standing with each of her three Oz companions.

A set of five *Wizard of Oz* porcelain sculptures was created by Balint Kramlik, a Hungarian refugee who emigrated to the United States in the early 1970s. His particular fascination with the 1939 MGM film inspired him to produce the Oz series from his Kramlik Porcelain Studio in the early 1980s. The figurines were distributed exclusively through the House of Goebel and were limited to five hundred sets worldwide. *Courtesy Patricia E. Smith.*

"Judy Garland as Dorothy and Billie Burke as Glinda" (left) and "Judy Garland as Dorothy" (right) musical figurines by Seymour Mann both played "Over the Rainbow" when wound. Available into the mid-1980s, the Dorothy/Glinda music box was marked 1981 while the Dorothy/Haunted Forest piece was marked 1983.

Beginning in 1984, Goebel Miniatures introduced its line of minute Oz character sculptures. Each of the hand-painted bronze figurines measured approximately 1 inch in height and was limited to an edition of five thousand. Sculptor Olszewski also created an Ozzy domed display setting for the miniatures which featured a yellow brick road winding up to the Emerald City. *Courtesy Goebel Miniatures.*

A set of four miniature figurines from the animated Cinar Films production of *The Wonderful Wizard of Oz* (1987) was marketed in Spain for the foreign 1988 release of the cartoon feature narrated by actress Margot Kidder. *Courtesy Chris Sterling.*

A 5½-inch Judy Garland as Dorothy porcelain figurine was another limited production "collectible" issued as one of Avon's Images of Hollywood Series in 1985. Other stars depicted in the series were Fred Astaire, Ginger Rogers, Clark Gable, Vivien Leigh and John Wayne.

Japan's enthusiastic reception of *Return to Oz* prompted the Heart & Heart company to manufacture 3- and 4-inch plastic jointed figures of four of the film's main characters in 1985.

Twenty MGM movie character likenesses comprised The Franklin Mint's 1988 *Wizard of Oz Portrait Sculpture Collection.* Intricately detailed in workmanship, each miniature figurine was crafted in Tesori porcelain and colorfully painted entirely by hand. The sculptures were accessorized by a custom-designed "Emerald City" display case, a certificate of authenticity and a mini reference library of information about the film. *Courtesy The Franklin Mint.*

In 1988, Presents of California introduced its line of widely distributed *Wizard of Oz* PVC figurines. The figures measured 3¾ inches in height and were likewise adapted by the company to produce keychains, Christmas ornaments, and revolving music boxes.

Four "Christmas Caroller" figurines of everyone's favorite characters were made available in autumn of 1989, produced by Kurt S. Adler, Inc. and distributed by Santa's World. *Courtesy Chris Sterling.*

Presents also produced six different Munchkin PVC figurines ranging in height from 1¾ inches to 2¾ inches.

Multi Toys' 4-inch Oz poseables were sold individually and in boxed sets in 1989.

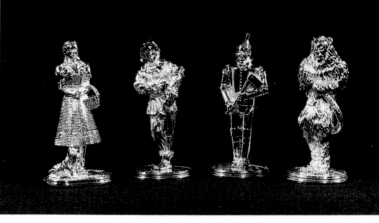

The Metropolitan Guild for Collectible Art's 1989 set of *Golden Anniversary Commemorative Wizard of Oz Figurines* stood approximately 4 inches high and was layered in 24K gold. The four different likenesses of the Oz film characters were exquisitely designed and sculpted down to the smallest detail by artist Carver E. Tripp. Each piece was engraved with the artist's signature and serial number and an official registration certificate guaranteeing authenticity accompanied each set.

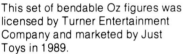

This set of bendable Oz figures was licensed by Turner Entertainment Company and marketed by Just Toys in 1989.

To commemorate the fiftieth anniversary of the MGM Oz motion picture in 1989, Dave Grossman Creations of St. Louis issued a highly detailed, limited edition set of cold cast marble figurines depicting Dorothy and her three companions as rendered by noted sculptor Michael Roche. The figures ranged in height from 5¾ inches to 8¼ inches, but were also available as

both miniature sculptures and Christmas ornaments. A year later, the line was expanded when the company marketed figurines of the Wizard, Glinda, and the Wicked Witch of the West. Independently of Dave Grossman, Roche went on to issue figures of a winged monkey and the Mayor of Munchkinland in 1992.

Well after the film's fiftieth anniversary had passed, The Franklin Mint continued to celebrate the magic of MGM's *The Wizard of Oz* by introducing a "Judy Garland as Dorothy" figurine in 1991. Crafted in fine bisque porcelain and decorated entirely by hand, the miniature sculpture stood approximately 8½ inches high. *Courtesy The Franklin Mint.*

Games and Puzzles

The first Oz-related game was commercially marketed in 1905 by Parker Brothers. *The Wogglebug Game of Conundrums* was inspired by Baum's "Queer Visitors From the Marvelous Land of Oz" comic character. Much of the influence ended with the name, however, as the game contained no further references to either Oz or the comic page with the exception of fifty-one "conundrum" or riddle cards and fifty-one answer cards— comparable to the puzzling perplexities posed by the intellectual insect! *Private collection.*

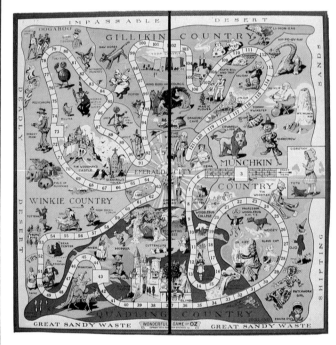

Parker Brothers' *The Wonderful Game of Oz* was one of the most visually satisfying Oz products ever published. The original 1921 editions of the game featured small pewter figural playing pieces representing Dorothy and her three companions. When the game was reissued in later years (the last issue being in 1939), the figurines were replaced by less costly wooden markers. Likewise, the full-color rule booklet was printed in black-and-white. The game also contained six dice that spelled out "W-I-Z-A-R-D" and a wooden dice cup. A Canadian version was issued by Copp-Clark, a company that published many of the Oz books as well. *Figural markers courtesy Chris Sterling.*

132

The vast array of jigsaw puzzles available across the country in the early 1930s included Reilly & Lee's *Little Oz Books With Jig-Saw Puzzles* set number one (1932). The box contained two softcover edition reprints of L. Frank Baum's 1913 *Ozma and the Little Wizard* and *The Scarecrow and the Tin Woodman* short stories and two full-color die-cut picture puzzles (thus comprising a box "full of fun"!). *Courtesy Rob Roy MacVeigh.*

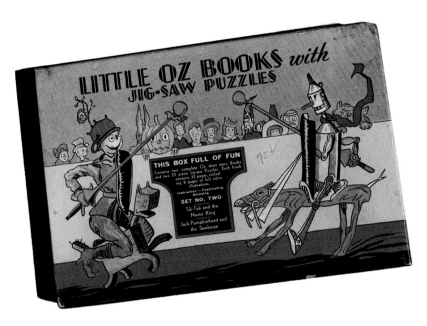

Reilly & Lee's *Little Oz Books With Jig-Saw Puzzles* set number two (1932) contained reprints of *Jack Pumpkinhead and the Sawhorse* and *Tik-Tok and the Nome King* booklets plus two cardboard puzzles of story scenes shown as double-page spreads in the booklets. *Courtesy Larry Schlick.*

133

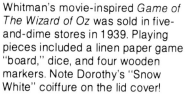

This 1940 *Wizard of Oz Card Game* was issued by Castell Brothers Ltd. of London to tie in with the release of the MGM film in Great Britain. The deck consisted of an instruction leaflet and forty-four playing cards (each a hand-tinted movie still) which, when aligned sequentially, provided a visual account of the famous story.

Whitman's movie-inspired *Game of The Wizard of Oz* was sold in five-and-dime stores in 1939. Playing pieces included a linen paper game "board," dice, and four wooden markers. Note Dorothy's "Snow White" coiffure on the lid cover!

Two boxed sets of picture puzzles "based on the motion picture *The Wizard of Oz*" were published by Whitman in 1939. Each set contained two puzzles adapted from Leason's illustrations for Whitman's *The Wizard of Oz Picture Book*. Illustrated above is the cover art and a puzzle from one set. The other box cover (not shown) depicted a scene from the book in which the Scarecrow is stuck on a pole in the middle of a river as the other characters look on from the safety of a raft *Puzzle courtesy Tod Machin.* (Only black-and-white box image available.)

E.E. Fairchild's *The Wonderful Wizard of Oz Game* was marketed in 1957 shortly after the Baum story characters became public domain. This game version of Dorothy's adventures featured a playing board similar to the 1921 Parker Brothers Game. Additional playing pieces included a spinner, instruction sheet/story synopsis, thirty-two playing cards and four wooden markers. A greatly reduced, cheaply made edition of this game was made available in the early 1970s.

Jaymar, a long-time puzzle manufacturer, issued a set of four frame-tray puzzles representing MGM movie scenes circa the early 1960s. (Absent from this picture is the puzzle entitled "The Plotters.") The puzzles were originally sold sheathed in cardboard slipcovers which framed each illustration.

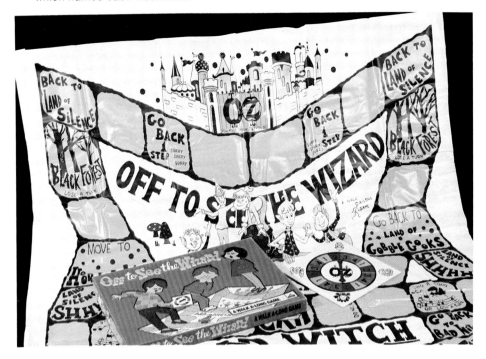

The Schaper Company's *Off to See the Wizard—A Walk Along Game* was copyrighted 1967 Metro-Goldwyn-Mayer as a tie-in with the prime-time cartoon show, however nowhere on either the box or the game contents were the animated characters apparent. Similar to the popular *Twister*, the game's players were human markers, physically moving about on a large vinyl "board." *Courtesy Chris Sterling.*

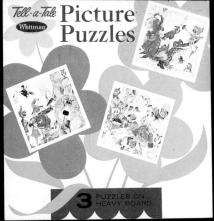

The Wizard of Oz, Alice in Wonderland and Peter Pan comprised a boxed set of 1967 Whitman "Tell-A-Tale" picture puzzles illustrated by George Buckett. Each puzzle was also sold separately in frame-tray format. Courtesy Rob Roy MacVeigh.

As one in a set of fairy tale puzzles marketed in canisters, H.G. Toys' Oz puzzle was also available from the 1960s to the 1970s in a box designed to resemble a storybook.

From the late 1960s to the early 1970s, Jaymar sold its Wizard of Oz picture puzzles repackaged in oversized boxes containing one hundred pieces. The Haunted Forest scene was concurrently issued in larger and smaller scale boxes.

Milton Bradley introduced its Off to See the Wizard Game in 1968 at a retail price of $1.68. The game consisted of a playing board, dice, five die-cut markers and a "Witch" disk.

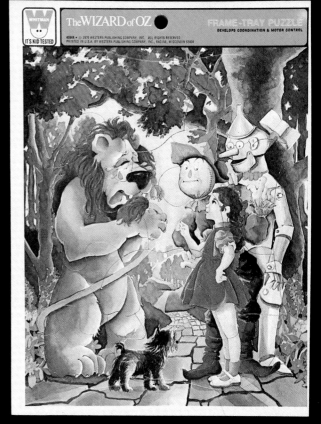

"From the MGM movie, an annual television favorite." Cadaco's *The Wizard of Oz Game* was published in tremendous quantity since Christmas of 1974. For the fiftieth anniversary of the film in 1989, it was reissued in a slightly revised box.

Whitman's 1976 line of *Wizard of Oz* activity books and products included two frame-tray puzzles depicting the beloved Baum characters. In addition to the example shown, the second puzzle illustrated the four friends glimpsing the Emerald City for the first time. *Courtesy Tod Machin; photo: JoAnn Groves.*

Several canisters of *Wizard of Oz* scene puzzles were made by the American Puzzle Company circa 1976. The character illustrations closely resembled the MGM film conceptions but were vague enough to avoid licensing infringement. *Courtesy Bill Beem.*

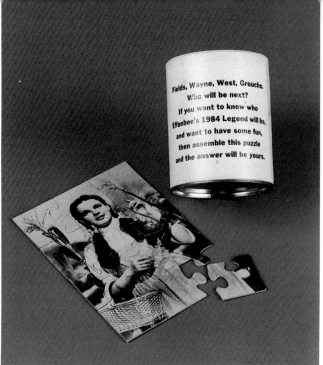

At least four different oversized frame-tray puzzles measuring 17" x 22" were printed in 1977 by Doug Smith Productions, Inc., two examples of which are illustrated. The other puzzles pictured the Wicked Witch threatening Dorothy, and Dorothy with her three Oz companions. All were licensed by MGM.

To publicize its 1984 Legend Series addition, Effanbee issued a small canister puzzle which, when assembled, revealed the latest celebrity to be immortalized by the doll maker. *Courtesy Tod Machin; photo: JoAnn Groves.*

Hallmark Cards published a *Wizard of Oz* "Children's Jigsaw Puzzle" picturing the traditional book characters circa 1983. *Courtesy Tod Machin; photo: JoAnn Groves.*

A 200-piece *Return to Oz* boxed puzzle was offered during the summer of 1985 as a send-away premium through Pringle's Potato Chips and Crisco Oil.

Two different *Return to Oz* frame-tray puzzles were printed in 1985 by Western Publishing's Golden Press. Western was also responsible for four 200-piece boxed puzzles similarly featuring color scenes from the Walt Disney film.

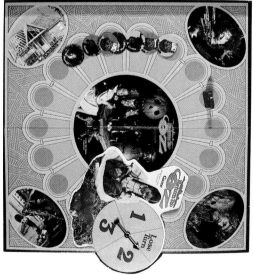

Western Publishing's Golden division marketed a *Return to Oz Game* in 1985. Game pieces included a playing board, spinner, four markers, and twenty-eight "ornament" disks.

Featuring the artwork of a poster retailed by the Norman James Company a year earlier, this 1990 *Wizard of Oz* jigsaw puzzle was one of several "Classic Movie Puzzles" produced by Milton Bradley.

Among the various *Wizard of Oz* items produced by Western Publishing Company in 1989 were several frame-tray and boxed jigsaw puzzles. In addition to those shown here, at least one other boxed puzzle was available depicting the poppy field scene as illustrated on the larger frame-tray puzzle.

Glasses, Cups and Mugs

Corning Glass Works, in connection with Sealtest Cottage Cheese, issued these *Wizard of Oz* tumblers as a weekly dairy promotion in 1939. Licensed as MGM movie tie-ins, the glasses were marked "© Loew's, Inc." and may also have been sold in five-and-dime stores. Logically, an eighth glass depicting "The Wizard" should exist to round out the set, however none have publicly surfaced as of this writing.

Libbey's 1953 Classics Collection was a series of drinking glasses issued in honor of famous books, including *Treasure Island, Moby Dick, Alice in Wonderland* and *Tom Sawyer*. One of eight such glasses issued, this particular tumbler commemorated the publication of Baum's *The Wizard of Oz* and was made in both eight-ounce and twelve-ounce versions.

Varied versions of the Swift Oz Peanut Butter labels and tin lids (1950s-1960s). *Courtesy Tod Machin; photo: JoAnn Groves.*

An alternate style of the Swift Oz Peanut Butter label is illustrated above. The 1970s reissue label was a stylized version of this picture.

A ceramic mug picturing the Tin Man and his cottage was one of many souvenirs offered during the 1970s at the Land of Oz Theme Park in Banner Elk, North Carolina.

Inspired by the original L. Frank Baum book characters, Swift & Company packaged their Oz Peanut Butter in a colorful assortment of decorative glass tumblers from about 1953 through the early 1960s. (The series also enjoyed a brief revival in limited areas in the late 1970s.) "Dorothy," "Toto," "The Scarecrow," "The Tin Woodman," "The Cowardly Lion," and "The Wizard" were marketed in glasses with fluted, wavy, or plain bases. The fluted base glasses were either marked "© Baum" or "© S & Co". The wavy and plain bottomed glasses were marked "© S & Co," although no priority is known.

A second series of six glasses was most likely issued by Swift after the initial main character sets. These tumblers pictured "Witch of the North," "Emerald City," "Wicked Witch of the West," "Flying Monkeys," "Winkies," and "Glinda" and were available in white and colored decal sets marked "© S & Co". A number of glasses from this series also had a starburst pattern on the bottom, however an issue priority is unknown. Note the original silver foil label on one of the tumblers.

In 1974, the Mann Theater chain issued a *Wizard of Oz* plastic cup with the purchase of a large soft drink. The cup's reverse provided a story synopsis and cast credits which curiously list George Cukor—not Victor Fleming—as the movie's director. (Although Cukor did provide integral touches to the film as an intermediary director during early production, he received no screen credit for his contributions.)

A set of early-1980s ceramic *Wizard of Oz* character mugs was made in Taiwan and copyrighted "J.S.N.Y." *Courtesy Tod Machin; photo: JoAnn Groves.*

As part of a circa 1975 promotion, Dunkin' Donuts issued a *Wizard of Oz* drinking glass. Available in orange-and-brown or buff-and-brown, the tumblers were marked only "© 1939 Metro-Goldwyn-Mayer, Inc."

Merely marked "© 1939 Ren 1966 MGM," this petite Oz mug dates from circa 1983. The reverse side proclaimed "M-G-M Presents Wizard of Oz" in addition to listing the four principal cast members.

A set of four limited edition "Land of Ahs" collector's glasses was distributed in 1984 by Kentucky Fried Chicken restaurants only within the state of Kansas. The glasses were part of a campaign to promote state tourism and each was marked "Collector's Series #1," as reissue sets were initially intended to have been produced.

A plastic mug manufactured by Whirley Industries, Inc. was available to fans attending *The Wizard of Oz Live!* during its 1989 tour. *Courtesy Chris Sterling.*

Krystal restaurants of Georgia, Alabama, Mississippi, Florida and Kentucky offered this set of fiftieth anniversary commemorative *Wizard of Oz* drinking glasses as part of a Coca-Cola summer drink promotion. From September 11 through October 21, 1989, a different one of the six glasses was available each week, free with the purchase of a sixteen-ounce Coca-Cola Classic for ninety-nine cents.

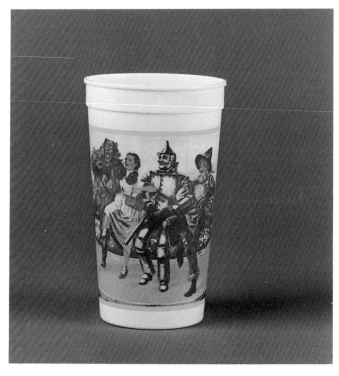

From July through September of 1989, Whataburger restaurants of Arizona, Tennessee, Oklahoma, Texas and Florida offered this *Wizard of Oz* fiftieth anniversary commemorative glass in conjunction with a Coca-Cola summer drink promotion. The glass was fifty-nine cents with the purchase of a large or jumbo Coca-Cola or free with any $3.50 purchase. A set of four was free with any $10.00 purchase.

A large plastic Oz drinking cup marked "1990; Sterling Products Inc." was a fiftieth anniversary Dairy Queen premium. *Courtesy Tod Machin; photo: JoAnn Groves.*

Scenes from four of The Hamilton Collection's *Wizard of Oz* collector plates adorned these ceramic mugs which were marketed through the company's Presents division in 1990.

Magazine and Newspaper Features

A May 1903 Malt-Sinew advertisement promoted both its home remedy elixir and Chicago's own *Wizard of Oz* stage celebrities, Montgomery and Stone, some five months after the show had moved on to New York. *Courtesy Michael Gessel.*

This circa 1903 magazine clipping depicted Anna Laughlin costumed in character as "Dorothy Gale" from the successful stage production. *Courtesy Michael Gessel.*

Denslow's SCARECROW and TINMAN in YUCATAN

Written and Illustrated by W. W. Denslow
Illustrator of The WIZARD of OZ and The PEARL and The PUMPKIN.

THE SHIPWRECKED CREW, guided by the Aztecs, wended their way toward the village near by.

"I am hungry," said the Lion, and the little brainless Aztecs edged away from him with startled looks.

The Scarecrow tried to reassure them by saying that he and the Tinman had traveled with the Lion for years and had not come contained some straw and a lot of comic songs, they elected him king of the festivities and decked him with a crown, sceptre and royal robes.

"Fun for all and all for fun," he shouted, as he took his seat upon the throne; "let joy be unconfined"

For many days the Scarecrow reigned as King of the Aztecs.

did not like to drag away his two friends who were having such a

to any harm.

"A Lion doesn't eat hay, straw or tin," the Aztecs replied, and hurried their march to the village, where they made haste to prepare a sumptuous feast for the Lion and the hungry shipwrecked crew; and everyone felt more safe and at ease when the former was well fed and had brushed the crumbs from his whiskers.

High carnival was held both day and night, and he, with the Tinman as his Prime Minister, led the songs and dances of these silly people.

There was only one anxiety among the Aztecs, and that was to keep the Lion well fed, and to do this they feasted him at all times. He could not go about but what the people spread breakfasts, lunches and dinners before him, and between meals they forced all sorts of dainties, candies and bonbons upon him. He had five o'clock teas, pink, blue and green; coffee before he got up and luncheons before he went to bed. They even woke him and gave him sandwiches at all hours of the night, until finally the poor Lion did not know what to do. He felt sleepy and uncomfortable all the time, he even talked in his sleep, and finally became so low spirited that he decided to run away from so much kindness, but royal good time.

Accident finally helped him out of his troubles, for one day, the Aztecs were giving a luncheon to the Lion on board of a new automobile boat that lay in the harbor.

The feast was over, and the laughing Aztecs were in a small boat to go ashore, when the unlucky Tinman tripped over the

SEA HORSE.

To do proper honor to the stranded guests, thrust upon them by the storm, a general holiday was declared, and the village was given over to feasting and jollity.

The Aztecs were a happy, simple people, who had only brains enough to enjoy themselves and devote all their energies to having fun; so it was no wonder that the Scarecrow was soon a great favorite with them.

When they examined the inside of his head and found it only motor, and with his foot turned on the electricity, so that the boat gave a leap and shot away from its moorings and over the water at lightning speed.

Beyond the lighthouse, out of the harbor, flew the swift sailing craft, taking the three friends away from their new companions in the winking of an eye, before they even had time to say good-bye.

"I was a great man in that country," said the Scarecrow sadly, "I wonder where we are going now."

Denslow's Scarecrow and Tinman in Bermuda

Written and Illustrated by W. W. Denslow
Illustrator of The WIZARD of OZ and The PEARL and The PUMPKIN.

THIS IS BERMUDA," said the Captain to the Scarecrow, and he waved his hand toward the shore as the great ship swung into Grassy Bay and the little steam launch came out from the Dock Yards for the mail.

"See these islands dotted about so handy," said the Scarecrow, " and notice on yonder shore, the dark green, dimpled here and there with white houses, the opal sky above, the deep blue and emerald green of the sea below, which all go to make a picture of enchantment that—"

Just here he went head over heels into the small boat among the mail sacks that the stewards were tossing into it. The Scarecrow was hit by one of the bags and being light, he was carried over the side with it.

There was a cry of dismay from the passengers when they saw their friend's mishap, but he was soon dug out from the mail bags by the Naval officer in charge and his jolly tars, and restored to the deck of the steamer, a little out of shape but still smiling.

As the good ship swung up to the dock at Hamilton, a joyous shout went up from the crowd on shore when they saw the Lion, the Scarecrow and the Tinman upon the upper deck, and in answer the three raised their hats in greeting.

"We must search these two men," said one of the Custom-house Officers, as the Scarecrow and the Tinman came down the gangplank.

"Have you any cigars or liquors concealed in that straw?" said another to the Scarecrow.

"This one looks like a regular tank," said the first officer as he sounded the Tinman by tapping on his body with a bit of chalk, " but he seems empty enough."

After a careful examination the two friends passed the Customs and went their way with the regulation chalk marks on their backs.

As the three went out upon the white street into the glad sunshine, their reception was a warm one. While the Scarecrow

and Tinman were greeted with a glad welcome, the Lion was a real hero. Soldiers and citizens alike, cheered and cheered again for the British Lion.

For all of which the Lion bowed and smiled his thanks, not knowing what it was all about. The Scarecrow made a neat speech to the crowd and the Tinman beamed from every part of his newly polished tinware.

The guests were soon hustled into a carriage drawn by four beautiful horses and away they went to view the wonders of the islands. They were first taken to the Palace to pay their respects to the Governor, who received them graciously and gave them the freedom of the islands. Then they visited Prospect and the Offiicers' Club, where a sumptuous luncheon was prepared. This was useless to the Tinman and Scarecrow, but the Lion did full justice to it and more than made up for his two friends' lack of appetite.

For days life was one continual round of pleasure for the three strangers. The clubs, soldiers, sailors and citizens joined in doing their utmost for their entertainment

One day when the Lion was sound asleep, the Scarecrow and Tinman wandered off by themselves, and by accident strayed into the soldier's tents at Warwick Camp.

"Here's a pretty hat," said the Tinman, as he tried on a helmet.

"And here is a coat that just fits me," said the Scarecrow.

"Let's dress up in these things just to show our respect for the British Army."

"Good idea," replied the Tinman.

To dress themselves in the uniforms hanging about was but the work of a few moments.

"Now, we will run off to the Lion and show him how grand we look," said the Scarecrow. And off the two jokers flew, down among the tents.

"Halt!" was the loud, stern command that came from a sentry on duty.

"Deserters," yelled an officer; "capture them, head them off!" From every tent there rushed red coated soldiers, who sprang in pursuit of the two fugitives. Dodge and run as they might, there was no escape, and the Scarecrow and Tinman were soon captured and marched off to the guard house surrounded by armed soldiers. The two jokers were thrust roughly in a corner, while

the soldiers crowded the room.

"So you will try to run away, will you?" said the officer, coming in at this moment. " Let me have a look at them. Who are they?" He was answered by a mighty roar, and a raging Lion sprang into the middle of the room through the open door. Terrified, the soldiers scattered in all directions. Away they flew through door and windows, and even up the chimney, while the long-legged Lieutenant led the van, making for the shelter of the woods, and for all the three friends know, he is going yet.

"Quick, on my back," said the Lion.

They did not need a second invitation and with mighty bounds the Lion tore down the white road leading to the hotel, bearing the happy Tinman and the Scarecrow on his back.

Evening had come and it was very dark when they reached the hotel by the water side and so they slipped in without being seen by anyone, and were soon taking off their regimentals.

"You were in a bad scrape, when I happened along," said the Lion severely. " You should behave with more respect toward the British army. Don't let it happen again."

"It is moonlight and there is a hop at the hotel to-night," said the Scarecrow. And they put on their full dress suits and went down to dinner.

QUEER VISITORS FROM THE MARVELOUS LAND OF OZ

Introducing the Scarecrow, the Tin Woodman and their Comrades

The Fairy Tale by L. Frank Baum   The Pictures by Walt McDougall

Copyright 1904 by L. Frank Baum

THE TIMES-DISPATCH

Comic Section

Richmond, Sunday, September 4, 1904

How the Adventurers Lost and Found Themselves

As day dawned the travelers from the Land of Oz looked over the sides of the Gump, which had been flying steadily all night, and descovered a large group of buildings just beneath them. "Stop!" called the Scarecrow to the Gump; "we have doubtless reached our destination. Please land us as gently as possible."

So the Gump fluttered down in the centre of a large enclosure surrounded by many rows of vacant seats, and the travelers alighted and assisted the Saw-Horse to reach the ground. Their first act was to place Jack Pumpkinhead upon the back of the steed, because the poor fellow, being somewhat carelessly made, can ride more safely than he can walk.

"Where are the United States?" asked Jack, looking around. "I don't see them anywhere."

"Where are the inhabitants of this strange place?" asked the Tin Woodman.

"Asleep, probably," returned the Scarecrow. "You mustn't forget that the unfortunate people who are made of flesh are obliged to sleep at night; and some of them forget to waken at daybreak. At least, that's what little Dorothy once told me.

"Let's go home," suggested the Gump, in a gruff voice; "this place is so strange it frightens me. Where are we, anyhow?"

No one could answer this question, and the Saw-Horse shivered and said: "I'm getting nervous myself. Suppose something should happen!"

"Something's got to happen," declared the Scarecrow; "it always does. Something happened the minute we arrived. Now follow me, and we'll explore this strange place."

So they walked around the enclosure and presently discovered a placard announcing a series of athletic games, which the learned Woggle-Bug read to his astonished friends. Also they chanced upon a number of dumb-bells, which delighted the Tin Woodman greatly. But while he amused his friends by lifting and juggling the dumb-bells a strange sound—like a roar of waters—was heard, and Wash White, a colored track roller, appeared upon the scene, still half asleep and not noting the group of queer people that stood in the enclosure. The Saw-Horse reared so wildly that he nearly dislocated Jack's wooden joints, and the others were equally startled at the sight of the wonderful jet-black Man of Flesh. Their cries caused sleepy Wash White to open his eyes, and what he saw made him yell with fear and run like the wind to the entrance, through which he escaped.

"What's the matter?" asked a Guard, who was trying his mettle.

"Malted 'nuff!" screamed Wash, trembling. "I's seed de debbil an' all his relations!"

In the meantime our friends from Oz had captured the track-roller and formed a procession to explore the place. For not one of the party could guess where they were, and all were more or less uneasy at being so soon lost in a strange land. As they reached the entrance to the enclosure the Guard, trying hard not to believe in Wash White's "dabbils," advanced with drawn club and chattering teeth and commanded them to halt.

At that instant the truth burst upon the Woggle-Bug, who cried in a loud voice: "I know where we are!"

"Where?" asked the Scarecrow, and the Woggle-Bug leaned close to his ear and said something in a whisper.

"Oh, yes!" exclaimed the Scarecrow, nodding his head cheerfully; "how stupid of us not to have guessed!" Then he turned to his friends and said: "Come on, comrades. We've found ourselves again."

L. FRANK BAUM.

Mounted on the Gump, the visitors from Oz arrive at dawn. The Scarecrow, the Tin Woodman, Jack Pumpkinhead and the Woggle Bug, with the Saw Horse, form the party.

"Will someone please tell me where we are?" asked the Scarecrow.
"It looks like an outdoor gymnasium," declared the Woggle Bug.

"I wonder," said the Scarecrow, "if all American belles are dumb?"
"They're amusing, anyhow," said the Tin Woodman.

The Track Roller arrives on the scene, and startles the visitors by his strange appearance.

But is frightened away by the Woggle Bug.

"Let's form a procession and explore this remarkable place," suggested Jack Pumpkinhead.

At this moment the wise Woggle Bug discovers their whereabouts. The question is:
"Where did they land?" (See prize announcement. What did the Woggle Bug say?)

Opposite page:

Between September 4, 1904 and February 26, 1905, L. Frank Baum scripted twenty-six plots of "Queer Visitors From the Marvelous Land of Oz," a full-color Sunday comic page as inspired by characters appearing in his book *The Marvelous Land of Oz*. To heighten interest in the Oz comic, many newspapers participated in the "What Did the Woggle Bug Say?" contest in which adept readers deciphered the riddle posed by the "highly magnified, thoroughly educated" insect at the conclusion of each episode for cash prizes. The premiere page from September 4, 1904 is reprinted here. (The answer to the question in the last panel—"Where did they land?": Stadium Athletic Field, Louisiana Purchase Exposition.) *Courtesy Michael Gessel.*

This page:

A full-page sheet of thirty "Queer Visitors From the Marvelous Land of Oz" cutout comic playing cards was most likely published in the *Philadelphia North American* circa 1904. *Courtesy Dede Schaeffer.*

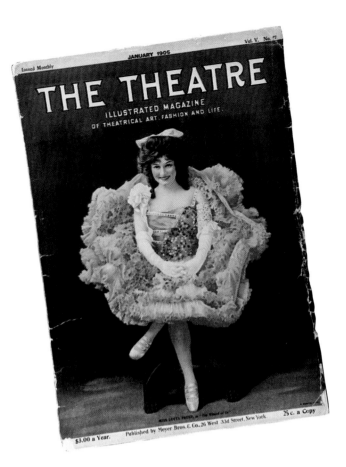

Wizard of Oz stage star Lotta Faust made an engaging cover subject dressed in character for *The Theatre* magazine's January, 1905 issue. *Courtesy Jane Albright; photo: JoAnn Groves.*

Typical of the magazine publicity given the Oz Film Manufacturing Company's "photo extravaganzas" was this 1915 advertisement from *The Moving Picture World.* Giving theater owners every possible opportunity to exploit the Oz productions, the company listed an array of accessible promotional materials. *Courtesy Audrea Cohen; photo: Myles Cohen.*

By arrangement with Reilly & Lee, the George Matthew Adams newspaper syndicate serialized many of L. Frank Baum's Oz books, beginning with *The Land of Oz* in early 1919. (Various papers across the country carried the feature as late as 1928.) Other Sunday installments of "The Wonderful Stories of Oz" included consecutive chapters from *Ozma of Oz, Dorothy and the Wizard in Oz, The Emerald City of Oz, Tik-Tok of Oz* and *The Scarecrow of Oz.* The earliest pages reproduced John R. Neill's book illustrations; later chapters pictured original drawings by an unidentified artist. Additionally, the *Cleveland Plain Dealer* sponsored a weekly contest in which a Baum Oz book was awarded to the juvenile author of the most original Oz story.

Gimbel Brothers promoted the Oz festivities held on the fourth floor of their Philadelphia store's toy department via a full-page ad taken out on November 20, 1920 in an unidentified newspaper. This pre-Christmas extravaganza took place six months after L. Frank Baum's death the previous May. The parade of characters at the page bottom was derived from Neill's endpaper design for 1920's *Glinda of Oz* book.

Wally and the Comical Lion, two characters syndicated in the *Los Angeles Times* funnies, presented a "Land of Oz" game in the paper's December 16, 1928 comic section—with "apologies to Frank Baum." *Courtesy* The Baum Bugle.

A number of motion picture periodicals published previews or reviews of Larry Semon's silent screen version of *The Wizard of Oz* in June or July, 1925. The French *Mon Ciné* publicized the film through this full-page illustrated feature.

Sample strips from "The Wonderland of Oz." The feature was syndicated in 443 daily black-and-white episodes (Monday through Saturday) in several United States papers as well as at least three Canadian papers from May 1932 to October 1933. The comic relayed the plots of *The Land of Oz*, *Ozma of Oz*, *The Emerald City of Oz*, *The Patchwork Girl of Oz* and *Tik-Tok of Oz* as written by L. Frank Baum and newly illustrated by Walt Spouse (though heavily patterned after John R. Neill's conceptions). Between 1938 and 1940, Dell Publishing revived the strip series as part of The Funnies comic books. For these reprints, the comics were colored and much of the lengthy text was supplanted by character dialogue "balloons." *Private collection.*

The first issue of *Meglin Kiddie News*, appropriately enough, publicized the first film in a proposed series of features produced by talent school director Ethel Meglin and showcasing her gifted young protégés. Their 1933 film, *The Land of Oz*, "starred" Maryeruth Boone as Dorothy and had its debut at the Fox Wilshire Theater in Los Angeles on February 25th. The picture, also known as *The Scarecrow of Oz*, was scheduled to be shown the following April 1st at the Meglin Pasadena Studio branch. *Courtesy Rita Dubas.*

The front page of the *Worcester Telegraph* radio and screen section for Sunday, October 1, 1933, reminded listeners to tune in to the new "Wizard of Oz" program sponsored by Jell-O gelatin and broadcast by NBC radio three times a week. The show aired from September 25, 1933 to March 23, 1934.

Judy Garland appeared on the cover of *Modern Movies* magazine for its March, 1939 issue wearing a dress created for her by *Oz* costume designer Gilbert Adrian. As part of the overall publicity the film would receive, Garland was featured in a variety of fashion photos and layouts dressed in a host of Adrian outfits inspired by the actress.

"MGM Risks $3M on 'Wizard of Oz'" boasted the *Des Moines Sunday Register* for July 2, 1939. The rotogravure section illustrated several exclusive Kodachrome publicity portraits of the movie's star players.

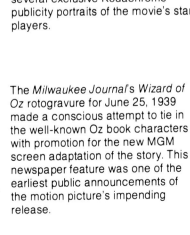

The *Milwaukee Journal*'s *Wizard of Oz* rotogravure for June 25, 1939 made a conscious attempt to tie in the well-known Oz book characters with promotion for the new MGM screen adaptation of the story. This newspaper feature was one of the earliest public announcements of the motion picture's impending release.

The *Chicago Sunday Herald & Examiner* publicized the forthcoming *Wizard of Oz* on the front page of its July 16, 1939 *Screen and Drama* section.

"'The Wizard of Oz' Makes the Movies" appeared in the *St. Louis Post-Dispatch* on July 16, 1939.

This full-page Sunday color comic advertisement primed youngsters—and their parents—for the excitement awaiting them at their local theater. An estimated twenty-nine newspapers in twenty-one cities circulated this feature in August 1939. Similar artwork was also used in magazine ads for specific "boy" and "girl" publications of the day.

A number of scene stills such as this portrait of Judy Garland were granted exclusive status through sparing distribution to select newspapers across the country in 1939.

Clever "Coming!" teaser ads were published by newspapers nationwide in the weeks prior to the August, 1939 release of The Wizard of Oz.

Among the earliest magazine coverage of *The Wizard of Oz* was a making-of-the-movie article in *The Family Circle* for July 21, 1939 (left). A favorable review largely praising Bert Lahr's Cowardly Lion appeared in the magazine's September 15, 1939 issue (right).

Judy Garland and Ray Bolger attempt to tame a cantankerous apple tree in an exclusive Kodachrome publicity still that served as the cover of the *New York Sunday Mirror* magazine section for August 20, 1939.

For its August 15, 1939 issue, *Look* magazine ran a "New Movie Preview" of *The Wizard of Oz* consisting of numerous color and black-and-white photos spanning four full pages.

Life magazine's August 28, 1939 issue featured an exclusive *Wizard of Oz* movie display ad. Well over a month earlier, *Life* had devoted an entire two pages to color photos from the film entitled "Dazzling Brilliance Marks MGM's Color Version of *The Wizard of Oz*" in its July 17 issue.

The *Oz* ad which ran in the August 26, 1939 issue of *The Saturday Evening Post* was an amalgam of publicity stills specifically hand tinted for the magazine's promotion.

Altoona, Pennsylvania's local merchants tied in with the town's September 1, 1939 premiere of *The Wizard of Oz* by advertising their wizardry in wares in a special combination announcement and coloring contest that appeared in the *Altoona Mirror's* August 31st edition. The format for the Ozzy "Back to School" layout was published in the film's campaign book and was employed by many newspapers across the country.

Standard newspaper advertisements of the day proclaimed *The Wizard* as being the "Miracle Picture of 1939." Note the semi-nude dancing girls at the ad's bottom!

Celebrity portrait artist Earl Christy adapted a publicity still for the *Wizard of Oz* cover of the August 1939 issue of *Screen Romances*. This advertising poster heralding the "novelization" of the screen story was intended for storefront display.

Atypical of newspaper announcements used to publicize the arrival of *Oz* to local theaters was this oversized advertisement in the *Altoona Mirror* on August 31, 1939—unusual in that it was printed entirely in red ink.

Minicam, a small format monthly magazine for camera buffs, featured an exclusive Kodachrome portrait of Ray Bolger as the Scarecrow on the cover of its August, 1939 issue. In addition, an interior article entitled "Hollywood Color Problems" detailed photographic obstacles posed during the filming of *The Wizard of Oz* and was illustrated with numerous behind-the-scenes stills.

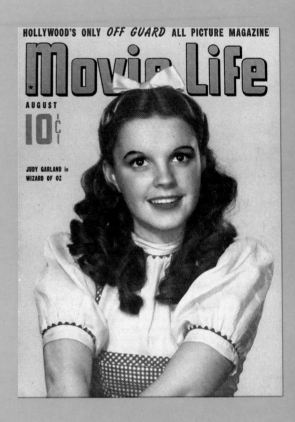

Movie Life magazine chose Judy Garland as its cover subject for August, 1939. This issue featured two pages chronicling the entertainer's "movie life" and two pages devoted to *Wizard of Oz* publicity. The cover portrait was from a photo sitting that produced a number of widely used publicity stills. *Courtesy the Baum Collection, Alexander Mitchell Library.*

Redbook magazine film critic Douglas W. Churchill selected *The Wizard* as "Picture of the Month" for September 1939. Churchill's plot synopsis and review was accompanied by scene stills and exclusive publicity Kodachrome transparencies which the magazine printed in red tone.

By the time this *Wizard of Oz* movie ad ran in the September, 1939 issue of *Parents'* magazine, the publishers had already recognized the picture with its honorary medal awarding the merits and quality family entertainment the film offered.

Below:
This particular advertisement incorporated three color publicity stills combined with Ozzy artwork. It appeared in the September, 1939 issues of *McCall's*, *Redbook* and *The American*.

The September, 1939 issue of *Ladies' Home Journal* featured a full-page color *Oz* advertisement. Ads identical in format ran in that month's issues of *Good Housekeeping* and *Woman's Home Companion* as well.

The Toronto *Star Weekly* for September 15, 1939 carried a hand-tinted cover portrait of Judy Garland as Dorothy and hailed the young up-and-coming actress as being "one of the brightest singing stars in the film firmament of Hollywood."

Judy Garland and Frank Morgan "endorsed" Certo jelly pectin—and their *Wizard of Oz* roles—in ads appearing in women's magazines and newspapers in October, 1939 (center). MGM's "Lion's Roar" magazine column publicized the new Oz production in August and September, 1939 (left and right).

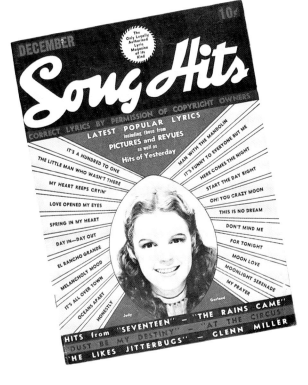

A *Wizard of Oz* issue of *Photoplay Studies* was distributed in September, 1939 for use by students enrolled in film appreciation courses. The booklet detailed how the MGM film was made through "interviews" with director Victor Fleming, producer Mervyn LeRoy and other production staff.

In follow-up to its October and November Oz features, *Song Hits* magazine chose Judy Garland as the cover subject for December, 1939. By the time this issue hit newsstands, Garland's rendition of "Over the Rainbow" had become number one in popularity nationwide.

161

Exemplary of the widespread international press exposure given MGM's *The Wizard of Oz* circa 1940 was the Danish *Hjemmet* magazine's two-page layout drawing attention to the American studio's expensive fantasy production.

The October 19, 1978 issue of *Scholastic Voice* magazine previewed the movie version of *The Wiz* for adolescent readers.

Republic magazine's June, 1985 issue featured a lengthy *Return to Oz* cover story. The article detailed the film's production and also included an overview of the evolution of Oz.

Postcards, Greeting Cards and Trading Cards

At least six different penny postcards illustrated scenes from the *Wizard of Oz* stage play circa 1902-08. One of the cards is clearly marked "Windeatt Photo Chicago" while another is partially marked "Byron NY." It is unknown whether some of the cards were originally available during the production's initial Chicago engagement or if the

"Broadway status" of the play company's transfer to the Majestic Theater in 1903 prompted printing of these publicity portraits. The postcard simply titled "Fred A. Stone" was also issued in a slightly larger format as published by W.J. Dwyer, New York. *Windeatt card courtesy Larry Schlick.*

Scene from "THE WIZARD OF OZ."

I have just seen "The Wizard of Oz." It is superb. Don't fail to see it if you get a chance. John.

CARTER & GUT, PUBLISHERS, N.Y.

A circa 1903 hand-tinted scene from *The Wizard of Oz* served both practical and promotional purposes as a penny postcard advertisement. The "hand-inked" inscription was actually printed on this card as made by Carter & Gut Publishers, New York. *Courtesy Dede Schaeffer.*

As an active participant in the "Queer Visitors From the Marvelous Land of Oz" promotional campaign, the *Philadelphia North American* distributed a set of six "Woggle Bug Lessons" cards. The "Jack Pumpkinhead" card (left) was number three in the 1904 series that described each character's origins and attributes on the reverse and announced, "He's in the Sunday *North American.*" *Courtesy Chris Russell and the Halloween Queen.* The *North American* also issued a different set of character postcards that same year (right), this time as a specific tie-in with the "What Did the Woggle Bug Say?" contest in connection with the "Queer Visitors" comic page. *Courtesy* The Baum Bugle.

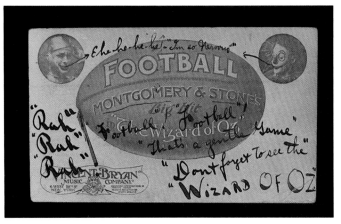

A sepia-tone postcard advertised Montgomery and Stone's "Football" song and comic routine in 1905. The musical number was one of several added to later runs of *The Wizard of Oz* to showcase the duo's antics. (The Vincent Bryan Music Company also published the accompanying "Football" song sheet at the same time.) The hand-inked inscription—"Ehe-he-he-he! I'm so nervous"—was a popular catch phrase from the play. Decades later, Stone would recreate the Scarecrow's high-pitched laugh when he assisted in the promotion of MGM's *The Wizard of Oz* on the June 29, 1939 "Good News" radio program. *Courtesy Cathi Dentler.*

Halloween greetings courtesy of a suspiciously familiar Scarecrow circa 1920s. The popularity of the Oz book series and this strawman's close resemblance to John R. Neill's illustration for the 1908 *Dorothy and the Wizard in Oz* copyright notice page make this postcard's unauthorized portrayal more than coincidental.

Thomas F. Gessner's illustration for a Denslow-inspired *Wizard of Oz* parade float used in the 1908 Mardi Gras festival was one in a series of postcards depicting the children's literature theme of the New Orleans Carnival, attenders of which included author L. Frank Baum.

A rose-tinted postcard scene from Chadwick Pictures' *The Wizard of Oz* promoting the 1925 film's premiere was printed by Exhibits Supply Company, Chicago. *Courtesy Jane Albright; photo: JoAnn Groves.*

A sky-high Denslow-inspired Scarecrow served as sentinel for the Enchanted Island at the 1933 Chicago World's Fair as depicted on this postcard. A similar Tin Woodman figure had also been erected at the fair and stood directly parallel to the Scarecrow (though not visible in this particular photograph). *Courtesy Dede Schaeffer.*

"The Talk of Hollywood" postcard was allegedly distributed only on the West Coast in 1939, calling attention to the impending release of Metro-Goldwyn-Mayer's latest screen achievement. *Courtesy Dede Schaeffer.*

THE TALK OF HOLLYWOOD

In the world's motion picture capital "The Wizard of Oz" is being heralded as Movieland's triumph of 1939. Filmed in Technicolor, set entirely to music and given realism throughout, it faithfully tells the story which has sold nine million copies since it was written by L. Frank Baum in 1900.

Judy Garland and Frank Morgan enact the leading roles in Metro-Goldwyn-Mayer's all-Technicolor production, "The Wizard of Oz."

This sepia-tone postcard was sent out by MGM in response to Judy Garland fan letters shortly before the August, 1939 release of *The Wizard of Oz*. The message appearing on the reverse read as follows: *"Dear Friend: Your inquiry concerning a photograph of Judy Garland has been received and is appreciated. Because of the tremendous volume of requests, the cost of complying is prohibitive unless partly defrayed by the applicant. We will be glad to send a 5" x 7" photo for ten cents; or an 8" x 10" size for twenty-five cents. Sincerely, METRO-GOLDWYN-MAYER STUDIOS."*

A set of twelve die-cut *Wizard of Oz* character valentines was issued by the American Colortype Company for 1940 and 1941. All of the cards were marked "Licensed by Loew's Incorporated from Motion Picture 'Wizard of Oz'" and each was designed with at least one easel tab that allowed it to stand independently.

JUDY GARLAND   METRO-GOLDWYN-MAYER

The British film publication *Picturegoer* routinely issued additions to its numbered set of movie star postcards in connection with the latest motion picture releases. In 1940, Judy Garland as Dorothy appeared on card number 1370 of the long-running series.

Three British cigarette cards advertised the MGM film circa 1940. The two *Wizard of Oz* scene cards also had a German translation on the reverse. The card picturing Judy Garland in a circa 1937 publicity portrait is significant in that the young actress described on back why her *Oz* role was her favorite to date. The "quote" was accompanied by a facsimile signature.

A series of souvenir postcards available at Banner Elk, North Carolina's Land of Oz in the mid-1970s were blatantly based on familiar MGM movie stills while concurrently providing a glimpse of the theme park's attractions. *Courtesy Dede Schaeffer.*

169

American Greetings offered a combination birthday card and game "inspired by the well-loved Frank L. (sic) Baum classic" in 1975 (left). By 1980, the game was newly illustrated and presented as a valentine (right). Also at this time, American Greetings marketed a boxed set of Oz valentines using the same style characters. *Courtesy Cathi Dentler.*

This circa 1977 Hallmark valentine was actually a six-page booklet providing activities such as a maze, connect-the-dots and a word search. *Courtesy Cathi Dentler.*

A *Wizard of Oz* boxed note card set printed in 1981 by American Greetings.

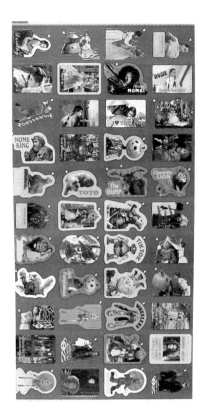

In 1985, veteran trading card company, Topps, issued a set of forty-four *Return to Oz* cards sold in individual packages containing six different cards and a stick of bubblegum. The cards featured peel-off character stickers on back and were also sold as complete sets in clear plastic boxes. An uncut sheet of cards is illustrated above left; the stickers printed on the cards' reverse are illustrated above right.

A series of twenty-five British *Return to Oz* collector's cards was issued in 1985 by English manufacturer Total Oil. Also distributed was a booklet containing a synopsis of the film with corresponding spaces for mounting the cards.

171

Since the early 1980s, Hallmark has recognized the familiarity and sentimentality of *The Wizard of Oz*—as is apparent from the wide variety of Ozzy greeting cards produced by the company for virtually every occasion!

Six different *Wizard of Oz* movie illustrations appeared on Fuld's boxed assortment of 1987 valentines.

Cleo marketed a boxed set of Oz valentines in late 1988 for Valentine's Day 1989. Each of the thirty cards featured a color frame from the classic MGM film.

In 1989, the Norman James Company, Ltd. of Canada offered both black-and-white and color scenes from the MGM motion picture in the form of sixteen different oversized cards. Measuring a full 8" x 10", each card carried the official *Wizard of Oz* fiftieth anniversary logo and contained an accompanying scene synopsis on the reverse.

Similar to the Cleo valentines, Pacific's 1989 *Wizard of Oz* trading cards featured a different color scene "from the original 1939 film" on each of the 110 cards in the set. The complete series was packaged in specially boxed sets in addition to being sold ten cards to a pack. A sign of the times, however, no sticks of bubblegum were included!

Popshots, Inc. offered several Ozzy "pop-up" and "slide" greeting cards as a novel means of sending birthday and get well wishes (1989 and 1990).

In 1990 and 1991, Paper House Productions printed seven different die-cut cards depicting full-color images from the 1939 Oz motion picture. Each card contained a corresponding narrative on the back and, together with a mailing envelope, was enclosed within a protective plastic sleeve.

This full-color, die-cut Wizard of Oz "Stand-Me-Up!" card was one of several different movie and movie star cards marketed by Triangle Enterprises in 1990. Each card came replete with a mailing envelope and an easel tab on back that allowed it to stand on its own.

A publicity postcard was distributed in early December of 1990 as announcement of "a heart-warming...movie inspired by...the author of America's favorite fairytale, The Dreamer of Oz: The L. Frank Baum Story." The two-hour television production aired as a December 10, 1990 holiday special on NBC.

Posters and Lobby Cards

The American Seating Company's Oz poster, circa July, 1929, was one of the earliest Oz product endorsements. Perhaps to appeal to educators and school children, an attempt was made to "humanize" the popular Scarecrow and Patchwork Girl characters—in spite of their familiarity and the fact that similar advertisements featured the traditional book characters.

The colorful, original 1939 movie theater insert poster for MGM's *The Wizard of Oz* measured the standard 14″ x 36″.

Miniature posters unto themselves, these lobby cards measured a standard 11″ x 14″ and were used during the initial release of *The Wizard of Oz* in 1939. Like most lobby cards used for promoting films of the day, the *Oz* set consisted of one title card and seven hand-tinted scene cards to be displayed in theater foyers and lobbies to offer patrons a glimpse of the story that awaited their viewing enjoyment. *Private collection.*

The original 1939 midget window card poster for *The Wizard of Oz* measured 8" x 14". Trimmed from the top of the example shown here is the blank area which allowed theater owners to imprint their own specific play dates and times. *Courtesy Tod Machin; photo: JoAnn Groves.*

A large poster for the circa 1940-46 French release of MGM's *Oz* measured 47"x 63", a size standard for many French posters. The artwork by "Grinsson" was typical of the style used to promote the film in the foreign market. *Courtesy Camden House Auctioneers.*

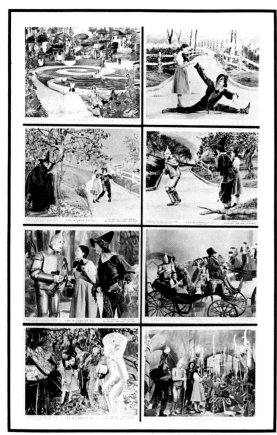

Eight hand-tinted movie stills made up the set of 8" x 10" lobby cards printed for British theaters. As the cards were marked "U" for general audiences, they were either issued after the repeal of the "A" (adults only) censorship ban in 1940 (due to Margaret Hamilton's menacing witch being deemed too frightening for children!) or in December, 1945 when the film enjoyed its English re-release.

Opposite page:

"It's Metro-Goldwyn-Mayer's Technicolor Triumph!" extolled the original 1939 half-sheet posters (22" x 28") for *Oz*. Top poster courtesy Audrea Cohen; photo: Cinema Art.

One of a set of unusually colored and interpreted Mexican lobby cards, this *El Mago de Oz* poster advertised the 1939 "grandiosa produccion de Metro-Goldwyn-Mayer." Each of the 12½" x 16½" cards in the set illustrated a different black-and-white movie still. *Courtesy Tod Machin; photo: JoAnn Groves.*

Another large format Mexican lobby card, circa late-1940s to mid-1950s, was one of eight similar cards issued after the initial Mexican film release. (Note the emphasis on Judy Garland and her trademark song, "Tras el Arco Iris.")

A beautiful 14" x 18¾" poster was used to promote the initial Belgian release of *Le Magicien d'Oz* circa 1946. Unlike the original shown here (marked "Imprimé en Belgique" and "Imp. L. & H. Verstegen, Bruxelles"), recent reproductions of the poster, which measured slightly larger, were simply marked "Printed in Belgium."

180

Half-sheet posters for the 1949 "Metro-Goldwyn-Mayer Masterpiece Reprint" measured 22" x 28". Shown here are both "Style A" and "Style B," the two different variants made available.

The triumphal entry into the Emerald City.

The Tin Man, the Cowardly Lion and the Straw Man — in disguise—prepare to attack the witch's castle.

The Wizard of Oz departs--for his old home in Kansas.

A lion acts tough in the Haunted Forest—until a little girl proves he's really a coward.

The evil witch plans a trap for two innocent travelers in the Land of Oz.

A warning from The Witch—but the travelers continue on their way to the Emerald City.

Dorothy wipes the Cowardly Lion's tears away!

The theater promotional package for the 1949 *Wizard of Oz* reissue included a new set of eight lobby cards to be used for display purposes. Unlike the original 1939 set, the hand-coloring for these particular cards was done with glaring inaccuracy. Note, for instance, Dorothy's blackened ''ruby'' slippers as well as the color of the famous ''yellow'' brick road! (Some variants of these cards were marked ''An MGM Silver Anniversary Picture'' across the top.)

Similar in many respects to that used for the original 1939 release, this window card poster provided vivid advertisement for the first American re-release of MGM's *Oz* in 1949. Normally measuring 14″ x 22″, the example shown here has been trimmed to a size of 14″ x 16″.

Having achieved international stardom in the years following her performance as Dorothy, Judy Garland's name and face were conspicuously highlighted on the 1949 reissue one-sheet poster (27″ x 41″). The portrait of Garland that appeared at the top was actually a shot from her 1944 film *Meet Me in St. Louis.*

Left:
The 1949 reissue insert poster for *The Wizard of Oz.*

Right:
Among the movie posters used for the 1955 *Oz* reissue was this newly-designed 14″ x 36″ insert.

"Let's go 'Over the Rainbow' with Judy in her greatest hit!" was the inviting message of the 1955 "Style A" half-sheet poster.

The 1955 reissue 30" x 40" movie poster for MGM's *The Wizard of Oz*.

Judy Garland's established star status was once again used as a device in promoting the 1955 reissue of *The Wizard*, as is apparent from this corresponding one-sheet poster.

For the American re-release of *The Wizard of Oz* in 1955, the MGM publicity department once again

Although the one-sheet poster for *The Wonderful Land of Oz* (1969) promised moviegoers would be "Ozified," the musical production based on Baum's *The Land of Oz* was lacking in overall quality of presentation and subsequently disappeared into obscurity. *Courtesy Bill Beem.*

This Portuguese one-sheet poster for *O Mágico de Oz* was undated but most likely from a re-release during the 1950s or 1960s since Judy Garland's name is prominent. (Though she was listed first, Garland's billing was of the same proportions as her co-stars during initial releases of the film.)

In 1970, a full-color *Wizard of Oz* poster was given away at Singer Sewing Machine outlet centers nationwide in conjunction with the company's sponsorship of the film's annual television broadcast that year. It was also distributed in a pre-folded state and was included as part of an early-1970s television offer that remaindered the MGM photo booklet, record, and songbook as a package deal.

This 1970 reissue window card poster (14" x 22") was for a select MGM Children's Matinee series of film re-releases. The artwork shown here also appeared on the other movie poster sizes issued as well as in newspaper advertisements.

A one-sheet poster for Filmation's *Journey Back to Oz*. This full-length animated feature film had a troubled history dating back to 1962. Despite a supporting cast of well-known celebrity voices, quality animation, and songs by veterans Sammy Cahn and James Van Heusen, the production was plagued with financial difficulties which delayed its American release until 1974.

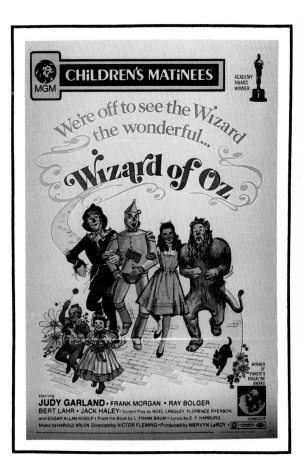

In 1972, MGM continued its Children's Matinee series with *The Wizard of Oz*. The newly-designed one-sheet poster is shown here.

A scene from *The Wizard of Oz* was included as one of eight lobby cards for *That's Entertainment*, a successful 1974 compilation of classic MGM production numbers produced by Jack Haley, Jr.

Despite a stellar cast and the reputation of the successful Broadway theater production on which it was based, Universal Studios' film version of *The Wiz* strayed so far from its original source that audiences in general found little resemblance between the 1978 box-office disappointment and previous Oz interpretations. The movie's one-sheet poster is illustrated here.

In 1976, a rock-and-roll interpretation of *The Wizard* was filmed and released in Australia, simply titled *Oz*. For its American release the following year, the film was retitled *20th Century Oz* as indicated on the *R-rated* one-sheet poster.

Artist John Trull designed this circa 1976 *Wizard of Oz* poster which was later adapted for fabrics such as tea towels and bed linens.

This circa 1980 Australian daybill poster touting "the happiest film ever made" measured 13" x 30".

A circa 1980 British quad poster, measuring 30″ x 40″, advertised MGM's *The Wizard of Oz* and *Tom Thumb* motion pictures. It was printed in England by Lonsdale & Bartholomew (Nottingham) Ltd.

"The Wicked Witch of the West wants YOU to clean up this room NOW!" threatened this 1984 Warren Siegmund poster. A slight variant was made available at the same time through a *TV Guide* offer in some regions of the United States. Those examples featured a border illustrated with silhouettes of Munchkins, the cyclone, the ruby slippers and other movie icons.

The Spanish one-sheet poster for *El Mago de Oz* from a circa 1982 reissue of the MGM film.

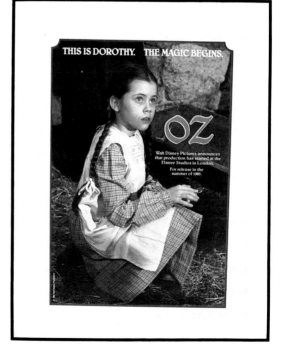

In 1984, the Disney Studios issued *Oz* pre-production posters to create interest in its new movie prior to the film's title change to *Return to Oz*. Fairuza Balk, a Canadian child actress, brought both sincerity and sensitivity to her portrayal of Dorothy.

Left:
A variant of the 1985 *Return to Oz* one-sheet theatrical poster—minus the "PG" rating—was used nationwide by Waldenbooks to publicize both the film and related Oz book titles. An identical lithographed edition of five hundred prints signed by artist "Drew" was primarily available to the film's production staff and crew.

Right:
The 1985 *Return to Oz* Australian daybill poster combined the British design artwork and the American "If there's one thing you must do this summer..." slogan. *Courtesy Tod Machin; photo: JoAnn Groves.*

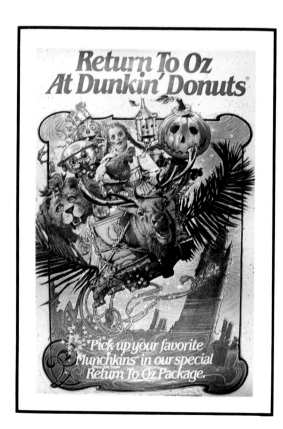

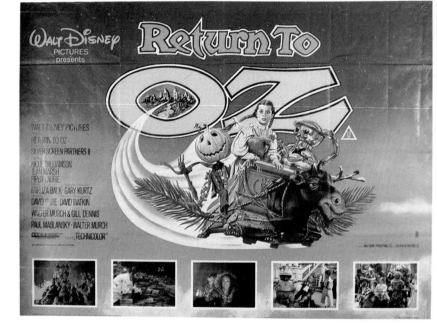

An enormous 40" x 60" window display poster advertised Dunkin' Donut *Return to Oz* "Munchkin" donut hole promotion in 1985.

The British 30" x 40" poster for *Return to Oz* was printed in England by "Londsdale & Bartholomew Ltd. Nottingham" in 1985. Unlike its American counterparts, this poster illustrated photo scenes from the movie and recommended viewers "read the Target paperback." *Courtesy Tricia Trozzi.*

A nightmarish 20" x 28½" Japanese poster depicted many of the more disturbing images seen in Walt Disney Pictures' *Return to Oz.* *Courtesy Tricia Trozzi.*

In an effort to boost sales, the *Return to Oz* video release poster emphasized that the film was direct from its (unsuccessful) 1985 theatrical release. *Courtesy Tod Machin.*

Circle Sports Ltd.'s 1985 *Return to Oz* poster booklet folded open into a 22½" x 33" modified version of the British movie theater poster (both sides shown). *Courtesy Tricia Trozzi.*

One of eight *That's Dancing!* lobby cards featured a scene from *The Wizard of Oz.* A major focus of the press campaign for Jack Haley, Jr.'s 1985 compilation of MGM film clips was the inclusion of an extended and wildly athletic version of Ray Bolger's song and dance, "If I Only Had a Brain."

This poster advertised the first in a series of "Graphic Novels" written and illustrated by Oz devotee Eric Shanower. The artist/author followed *The Enchanted Apples of Oz* (1986) with several other original Oz titles published in comic book format including *The Secret Island of Oz, The Ice King of Oz, The Forgotten Forest of Oz* and *The Blue Witch of Oz.*

Shown here is the colorful poster issued by MGM/UA Home Video during 1985-86 for use in stores nationwide in promoting its *Wizard of Oz* videotape—at the new low price of $29.95.

London's Royal Shakespeare Company production of *The Wizard of Oz* played at the Barbican Theater during Winter 1987-88. The musical was largely influenced by the 1939 MGM movie (even restoring the "Jitterbug" song) but retained Baumian touches as well. The advertising poster here promoted the play as did an alternate style subway poster. *Courtesy Michael Gessel.*

Right:

The *Wizard of Oz* videotape once again was repackaged for MGM/UA's "Fiftieth Anniversary Edition" which was released on August 15, 1989—this time at yet an even lower price of $24.95 ($19.95 after a Downy rebate!). The in-store advertising poster is shown here.

MGM/UA Home Video distributed this promotional display poster in conjunction with the *Oz* videotape's repackaging in 1988.

The *Wizard of Oz Live!* world arena tour production poster also advertised the show's commercial sponsors: Purina Dog Chow and Downy Fabric Softener (1989). *Courtesy Tricia Trozzi.*

Below:

MGM's *The Wizard of Oz* was once again released to theaters in 1989 in conjunction with its fiftieth anniversary celebration. As such, a new one-sheet poster was issued to provide advertisement for the film's many limited engagements across the country.

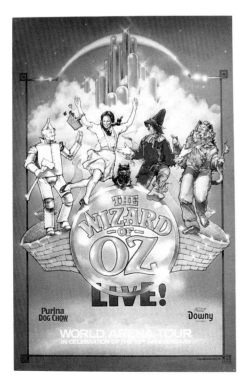

195

Left:

Though resembling a movie theater advertising poster, this print produced by the Norman James Company, Ltd. of Canada was marketed for retail sale in 1989.

Right:

A vivid poster announcing the impending December 10, 1990 air date of the *Dreamer of Oz* television movie was distributed among school teachers to incite student interest in reading and writing with the passion possessed by author L. Frank Baum (portrayed in the biographical film by actor John Ritter). *Courtesy Tod Machin; photo: JoAnn Groves.*

A commemorative Oz print marketed by Art One Images of California in 1989 was derived from a serigraph done by artist Melanie Taylor Kent.

For the 1990-91 television season, DIC Animation created a *Wizard of Oz* cartoon program featuring the characters, songs and background scoring from the 1939 film. Though incorporating voice imitations of the original actors and animation that was a cut above the usual Saturday morning fare, the series lasted just one season. Later that year, Turner Home Entertainment issued four of the show's episodes on two videocassettes which were announced through an advertising poster. *Courtesy Tod Machin; photo: JoAnn Groves.*

Publicity and Promotion

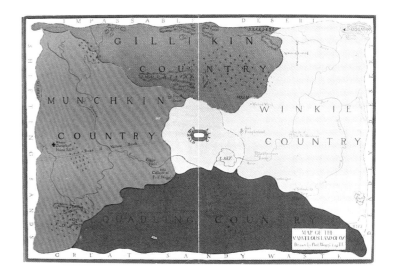

The Land of Oz map was first printed as one of the endpapers for *Tik-Tok of Oz* in 1914. (The other endpaper illustrated Oz and its surrounding countries.) This promotional giveaway (folded as made) was distributed in 1920 by publishers Reilly & Lee who would also reissue a black-and-white version of the map for a coloring contest seven years later. Students of Oz will quickly acknowledge the map's inaccuracies: the blue Munchkin country should be East, while the yellow Winkie country (home of the infamous Wicked Witch) should be West. The flyer's reverse depicted the official Flag of Oz.

New York's Majestic Theater issued weekly editions of its *Wizard of Oz* musical program. Contained within this printing for the week of May 4, 1903 was a plot synopsis, cast credits, and a musical agenda in addition to numerous contemporary advertisements for clothing, toiletries, and liquor.

The 1928 national tour of New York's Jean Gros French Marionettes' *Magical Land of Oz* presentation was advertised through the distribution of these two "Lucky Oz Pictures" printed by Reilly & Lee as bookmarks. The John R. Neill illustrations of the Scarecrow riding the Cowardly Lion and the Tin Woodman atop the Hungry Tiger were first published in 1913 as the endpapers for *The Patchwork Girl of Oz* and The Little Wizard Series.

Six months prior to the August 1939 release of MGM's *The Wizard of Oz*, Loew's Incorporated distributed this special stationery promoting "the greatest magic film ever to be made." The example illustrated here was printed for Maud Gage Baum, widow of author L. Frank Baum, while copies of the letterhead used by Loew's officials and theatrical booking agents carried the company's New York address for "further information." For the film's fiftieth anniversary in 1989, Turner Entertainment authorized the reproduction of a scaled-down version of the stationery, marked as such along the paper's bottom edge. *Courtesy Michael Gessel.*

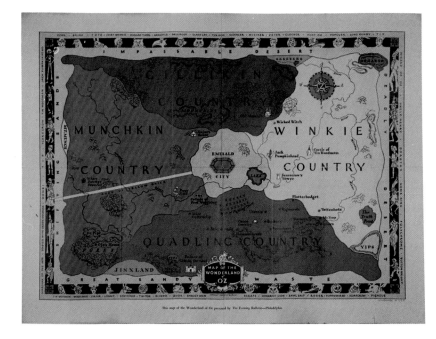

In sponsorship of the 1932 syndicated "The Wonderland of Oz" comic strip, Reilly & Lee printed Oz maps to be distributed to the comic's fans by newspaper offices. Through a "letter" from the Scarecrow as printed in the strip's sixtieth installment, readers were invited to send for the map by enclosing a two-cent stamp care of their newspaper. The characters bordering the map were drawn by the strip's writer and illustrator Walt Spouse and included several of Ruth Plumly Thompson's creations. The Munchkin and Winkie countries were inadvertently reversed on this map as well. *Courtesy Hake's Americana & Collectibles, York, PA; photo: Russ King.*

The *Wizard of Oz* "exploitation" book was enclosed as part of the overall packaging for the 1939 movie campaign pressbook. In addition to advertising theatrical materials such as banners, buttons, and life-sized cutouts, the promotional pamphlet provided ideas for gimmicks and contests designed to incite interest in the film. Two other sections included in the pressbook were the exhibitor's service sheet (a newsprint section containing prepared reviews and news features) and a section devoted to various theater ad mats for newspaper reproduction.

The front cover of the oversized 1939 *Wizard of Oz* campaign book illustrated the artwork used for the 14″ x 22″ window card poster while the back cover depicted a variety of other posters available to theater owners to aid in promoting ticket sales.

The August 14, 1939 edition of MGM's in-house *Studio News* publication was devoted almost entirely to *The Wizard of Oz*. In lieu of the availability of the official campaign pressbook, this oversized pamphlet contained prepared news stories and ads, and was mailed out to Loew's theater managers nationwide. The following evening, August 15th, *The Wizard* had its Hollywood premiere at Graumann's Chinese Theater. The original program for that screening featured a cover identical to that of the *Studio News*.

Several differently designed *Wizard of Oz* rayon advertising banners were available to movie theaters for rent in an assortment of sizes in order to aid the MGM film's promotional campaign in 1939. *Courtesy Audrea Cohen; photo: Myles Cohen.*

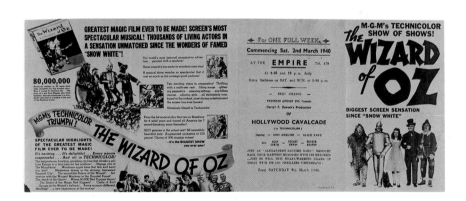

A lavishly illustrated handbill giveaway flyer measuring 5″ x 8″ folded open to a full 8″ x 20″—a mini poster and a piece of propaganda that surely stimulated interest in the 1939 release of "the biggest sensation since *Snow White*!" A sample copy of this handbill was inserted into each issue of the original campaign book folder.

Theaters across the country typically printed black-and-white flyers for *The Wizard of Oz* and other films of the day for the original 1939 engagements. Two such examples are illustrated.

An inexpensive souvenir given to patrons of Lebanon, Pennsylvania's Colonial Theater in August, 1939 was this small envelope of "magic sand from along the yellow brick road to the Land of Oz." *Courtesy Hake's Americana & Collectibles, York, PA; photo: Russ King.*

The Loew's theater chain distributed this *Wizard of Oz* edition of its weekly publicity flyer free to movie patrons on September 21, 1939.

Once World War II ended, international distribution of MGM's *The Wizard of Oz* could continue garnering first-time exposure in a number of foreign countries such as Austria, where, in 1946, an eight-page movie campaign book heralded *Der Hexer Von Oz.*

A much less elaborate and greatly streamlined revision of the original 1939 campaign package was issued to theater owners for the 1949 re-release of the MGM film. Nonetheless, the presskit offered gimmicks and promotions in addition to illustrating newly designed lobby cards and an assortment of other posters for use in publicizing *The Wizard of Oz.*

A vividly colored *El Mago de Oz* preview flyer announced the initial 1946 Spanish engagements of the fantasy film. *Courtesy Tod Machin; photo: JoAnn Groves.*

A small 3½″ x 5½″ color advertisement for *El Mago de Oz* was printed in Barcelona in 1946. *Courtesy Tod Machin; photo: JoAnn Groves.*

Somewhat small to be considered a poster, this 4″ x 11″ advertising card was most likely displayed in box-office windows and such during the 1949 reissue of *The Wizard*.

To help publicize its 1955 reissue of *The Wizard of Oz*, MGM again issued a new campaign pressbook. Included inside the package was a sample of the lively two-color heralds that could be purchased by theater owners with or without their own theater names, play dates, and co-features imprinted on the back.

Reproductions of four of Dick Martin's paintings for Reilly & Lee's *The Visitors From Oz* (1960) were used for bookstore display. The book was derived from Baum's 1904-05 comic page of similar title. In 1961, Martin likewise illustrated abridged versions of the first four Oz books, also published by Reilly & Lee.

Der Hexer Von Oz was a four-page program flyer for a German release of MGM's *The Wizard* circa the early 1960s.

Special in-store hanging cards promoting the March 15, 1970 television air date of *The Wizard of Oz* were displayed in Singer sewing outlet centers nationwide. Singer had sponsored this, the twelfth broadcast of the movie, and the company's extensive publicity surrounding the event helped it receive the fourth largest viewing audience for that week according to the Nielsen television rating system. *Courtesy Rob Roy MacVeigh.*

"Come With Us Over the Rainbow!" Encouraging handout flyers were available to theaters for distribution in connection with the 1972 MGM Children's Matinee reissue of *The Wizard of Oz.*

The brief two-page pressbooks issued for both the 1970 (left) and 1972 (right) Children's Matinee reissues of *The Wizard of Oz* nonetheless offered new publicity ideas, prepared reviews and announcements, newspaper advertisements, posters, stills, and lobby standees.

The cover of the original Broadway program for *The Wiz* prominently featured the artwork used in all advertising to promote the successful stage adaptation of L. Frank Baum's original story in 1975.

A *Wiz* record counter display advertised the 1975 Atlantic Records cast album of the "Super Soul Musical." *Courtesy Jane Albright; Photo: JoAnn Groves.*

The playbill cover for Broadway's smash hit *The Wiz*, August, 1976 edition. *Courtesy Cathi Dentler.*

The Wiz movie pressbook (1978) offered standard publicity devices such as various sizes of newspaper ads, cast photos, and a story synopsis. *Courtesy Cathi Dentler.*

This press sheet for a 1982 Spanish release of MGM's *El Mago de Oz* exhibited the one-sheet poster artwork on one side while providing film stills, story synopsis, publicity phrases, and cast and crew credits on the reverse.

A Japanese theater program for a 1955 release of *The Wizard of Oz* provided a synopsis of the film story illustrated with movie stills and drawings from a Japanese edition of the Baum book. The program was reprinted in 1984 by MGM/UA Entertainment Company.

The cover of a *Return to Oz* fold-out cast and credit list (1985). *Courtesy Tod Machin; photo: JoAnn Groves.*

The publicity presskit for *Return to Oz* contained a wealth of information designed to exploit the 1985 Walt Disney Pictures release to the fullest extent. The campaign folder was comprised of six black-and-white stills, a marketing kit detailing limitless promotional possibilities, a complete list of cast and crew credits and biographies of the film's major participants—including the late L. Frank Baum. *Courtesy Tricia Trozzi.*

A pop-up brochure issued by Del-Rey Books in spring 1985 announced the June publication of the *Return to Oz* screenplay novelization. The herald also hyped the feature film itself, as well as a variety of bookstore displays and Oz titles available from the publisher. *Courtesy Tricia Trozzi.*

An appropriate Oz tie-in was sponsored in 1985 by the Dunkin' Donuts chain in promotion of the restaurant's "Munchkin" donut holes, which were available in three *Return to Oz* carrying box assortments.

The box-office failure of Disney's *Return to Oz* in the summer of 1985 paved the way for a hasty transfer to videocassette just a few months later. This promotional yellow brick announced the video's release dates and served as a paperweight. *Courtesy N. Thomas Rogness.*

Two different British *Return to Oz* hanging mobiles for theater lobby display (1985). *Courtesy Chris Sterling.*

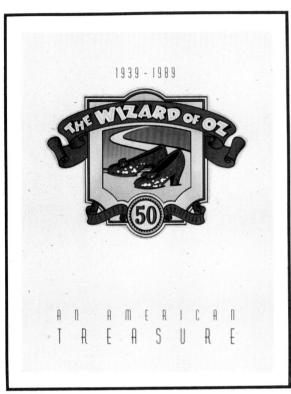

The Wizard of Oz: An American Treasure was a presskit issued by Turner Entertainment to promote the eventful fiftieth anniversary of the motion picture in 1989. Included inside the illustrated folder were facts about L. Frank Baum, stories surrounding the making of the movie, cast and crew credits, information regarding planned merchandise, and even trivia questions.

A deluxe souvenir program (left) detailed production of The Wizard of Oz Live!, a lavish arena presentation based directly on the MGM film in honor of its fiftieth anniversary. The musical toured seventy cities nationwide from March 10 to December 31, 1989. (right) The play's publicity pressbook contained photos and prepared biographies of the show's cast as well as other newsworthy promotional releases.

Prior to the August, 1989 release of its "Fiftieth Anniversary Edition" of *The Wizard of Oz* videotape, MGM/UA issued an impressive presskit as a prelude to an expansive $8.5 million promotional campaign. Included within the kit were print ad materials, film stills, press releases, a display banner, a newsletter, stationery, and biographies of the *Oz* stars.

An elaborate boxed presskit was distributed to video store owners and sales representatives by MGM/UA Home Video as a means of aggressively promoting its 1989 Fiftieth Anniversary Edition of *The Wizard of Oz* videotape. The array of things contained within the package included posters, press releases, display materials, and a ten-minute exploitation video featurette which brazenly extolled the *capitalistic* virtues of the film ("Somewhere over the rainbow a pot of gold and profits is waiting for you...!").

To aid video merchants in selling the Fiftieth Anniversary Edition of *The Wizard of Oz*, MGM/UA made colorful inflatable balloons available for in-store display. (The balloons were also used as promotional contest-related prizes.) Though the balloons themselves were identical, two slightly different styles of the cardboard baskets were printed. *Courtesy Tod Machin; photo: JoAnn Groves.*

With proof-of-purchase from Downy products, owners of the Fiftieth Anniversary Edition of *The Wizard of Oz* videotape could receive this five dollar rebate check from "The Royal Bank of Oz." The magnificent color graphics of the oversized checks were no doubt intended to *discourage* bearers from redeeming them!

In 1989, Dairy Queen celebrated both the Golden Anniversary of *The Wizard of Oz* and its own fifty years in business with an advertising calendar and coupon poster combination.

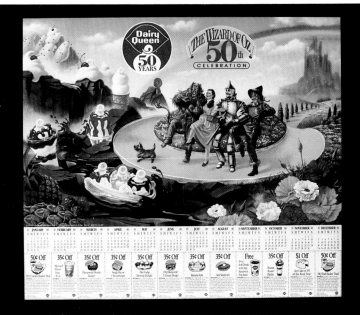

In conjunction with its *Wizard of Oz* drinking glass promotion in 1989, Whataburger restaurants distributed several children's "Fun Kits" as well as having four different decorated bags for its Kids Meal packs.

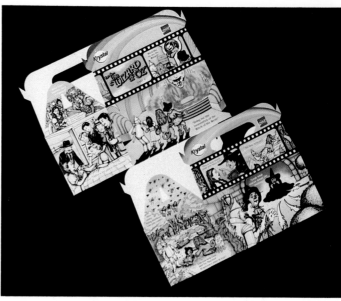

Part of the *Wizard of Oz* summer drink promotion sponsored by Krystal restaurants of Georgia, Alabama, Mississippi, Florida, and Kentucky was this paper tray liner-placemat and two different Kids Meal boxes (one of which is shown).

One of several dozen fiftieth anniversary licensees, Pfizer Laboratories appropriately used an MGM Tin Man likeness to endorse arthritis precautions and its anti-arthritic drug Feldene in brochures, magazines, newspaper ads, and television commercials. The brochure counter display is shown here, as is a special promotional digital Tin Man clock. *Courtesy Tod Machin; photo: JoAnn Groves.*

Turner Entertainment, in connection with DIC Animation, issued a special pop-up publicity folder announcing its *Wizard of Oz* Saturday morning cartoon program for the 1990 fall lineup.

Records and Sheet Music

M. Witmark & Sons published "Successful Numbers From the Musical Comedy The Wizard of Oz" in Denslowesque wrappers in 1902. Song sheets in this series were likewise available in different cover colors including dark green and gray. It was at this time that New York's Aeolian Company issued a player piano roll of "The Wizard of Oz: Selections by Paul Tietjens." (Tietjens was the show's musical composer.) *Courtesy Cathi Dentler.*

Sol Bloom Publishers printed "Sammy" in song sheet form in 1902. One of the interpolated numbers from *The Wizard of Oz* stage production, it was first sung by Lotta Faust, one of the original cast members. In later runs of the play, Faust's role of Tryxie Tryfle would be assumed by Grace Kimball, whose name and portrait would replace those of Faust on this music cover. *Courtesy Cathi Dentler.*

"When the Circus Comes to Town" as sung by actress Lotta Faust (playing Kansas waitress Tryxie Tryfle) in the stage production of *The Wizard of Oz* was the Sunday music supplement of newspapers nationwide for May 10, 1903. Within a matter of months, however, the song would be deleted from the show's program in favor of a new duet entitled "The Tale of the Cassowary."

"The Scarecrow From The Wizard of Oz" was a February 1, 1903 Sunday newspaper supplement depicting Fred A. Stone in the role for which he was fast becoming most renowned. Although the play had already been performed at New York's Majestic Theater for well over a week by the time this song sheet was printed in papers across the country, the photograph used on its cover was a publicity pose taken in Chicago for the stage debut at the Grand Opera House.

In 1904, Shapiro, Remick and Company of New York published "New Musical Gems From The Wizard of Oz" to showcase the variety of recently written numbers for the stage play's later-run performances. *Courtesy Michael Gessel.*

The sheet music to a love song entitled ''Dorothy'' was dedicated to actress Anna Laughlin (Dorothy of the *Wizard of Oz* stage show) and published in 1904 by Brooks & Denton Publishers, New York. Unauthorized and written solely to take advantage of *The Wizard*'s popularity, the song had no other connection to the musical production. *Courtesy* The Baum Bugle.

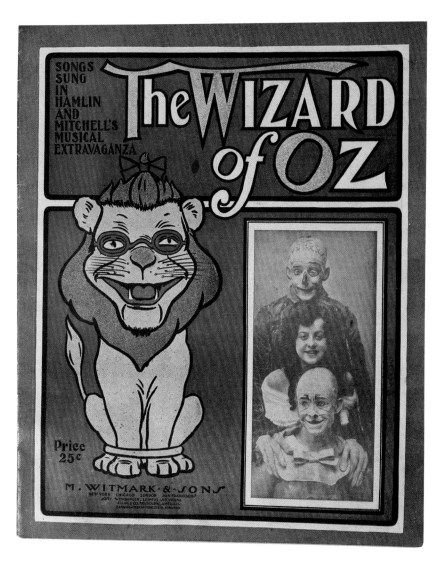

Victor's Monarch Records released Arthur Pryor's military band rendition of selections from the score of the *Wizard of Oz* stage play circa 1905. *Courtesy Larry Schlick.*

Songs Sung in Hamlin and Mitchell's Musical Extravaganza The Wizard of Oz was printed by M. Witmark & Sons. This eighteen-page folio contained words and/or music for nineteen songs dating between 1902 and 1905, three of which credited L. Frank Baum as lyricist. The front cover depicted Denslow's spectacled Cowardly Lion next to a publicity portrait of Montgomery, Stone and Anna Laughlin as Dorothy. The back cover was printed in two variations with either another green-tone photograph of the three actors or a copy of the play program. The songbook retailed for twenty-five cents and was most likely available in theater lobbies.

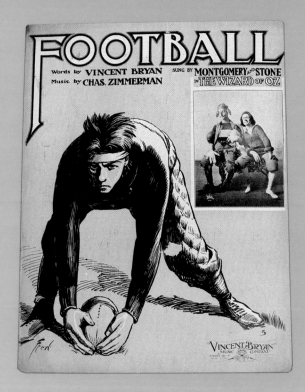

A relatively recent form of recreation, the sport of football was elevated to theatrical heights after a song and comic routine was added to *The Wizard of Oz* production in 1905. The "Football" sheet music was printed by the Vincent Bryan Music Company and pictured the comedic twosome of Montgomery and Stone in full uniform. *Courtesy Larry Schlick.*

Although L. Frank Baum's 1905 stage adaptation of *The Marvelous Land of Oz* was unsuccessful, M. Witmark & Sons printed *The Woggle-Bug*'s musical numbers and instrumental arrangements in songsheet form. The artwork for the sheet music covers incorporated illustrations by Ike Morgan (who pictured Baum's *The Woggle-Bug Book* that year), John R. Neill and Walt McDougall. This particular song sheet originally belonged to Matilda J. Gage, staunch advocate for the women's suffrage movement in the 1800s—and Baum's mother-in-law. A player piano roll for another of the production's songs, "My Little Maid of Oz," was published by the Aeolian Company. *Courtesy the Baum Collection, Alexander Mitchell Library.*

The accompanying Victor recording of the comic song "Football" was performed by Dan W. Quinn "with orchestra" about 1905. *Courtesy Larry Schlick.*

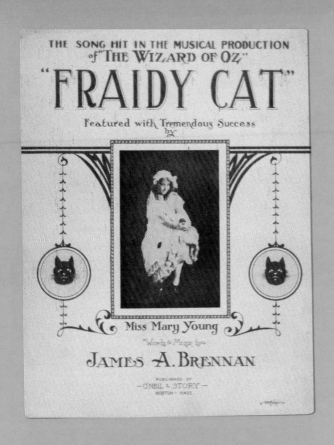

"Fraidy Cat" was an extraneous
song written by James Brennan for
later runs of the *Wizard of Oz* stage
play, at which time Dorothy was
portrayed by Mary Young. The
accompanying sheet music was
published in 1912 by O'Neil & Story
of Boston. *Courtesy Audrea Cohen;
photo: Myles Cohen.*

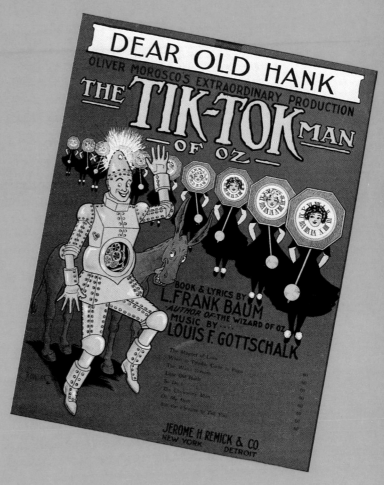

"Dear Old Hank" was one of eight
songs from Baum's favorable 1913
stage production of *The Tik-Tok
Man of Oz* to be published by
Jerome H. Remick & Company.
Other song sheet titles not listed on
the music's cover were "Folly! (The
Fool Song)," "Just For Fun," "The
Army of Oogaboo" and "Rainbow
Bride." Five of the songs published
by Remick also appeared in 1913
as a player piano roll through
Rythmodik, New York. *Courtesy the
Baum Collection, Alexander
Mitchell Library.*

"My Wonderful Dream Girl" sheet
music from *The Tik-Tok Man of Oz*
(1913) was one of several
interpolated songs for the stage
play written by Victor Schertzinger
and Oliver Morosco, the show's
producer. Other titles printed by the
Joe Franklin Music Company in
identical wrappers were "I Want to
be Somebody's Girlie" and "Oh
Take Me!"

In 1914 Jerome H. Remick & Company reissued "Ask the Flowers to Tell You" from *The Tik-Tok Man of Oz* in "Popular Edition" wrappers. The song was also released as a record on the Victor label. *Courtesy Michael Gessel.*

In July, 1939, Harry Link, of Leo Feist music publishers, issued five thousand complete musical orchestrations of the MGM *Wizard of Oz* production numbers to dance bands to advertise the potential song hits from the new motion picture. "Over the Rainbow" was also printed as a secular choral arrangement for church choirs.

"In the Castle of Glinda" from the *Tales From the Land of Oz* sheet music selections was published in 1932 by Schroeder & Gunther, New York. Intended as one in a series of children's piano exercises with an Oz theme, the composition was written by Irene Rodgers and the cover illustration was designed by Ruth Morterund. This songsheet remained in print as late as 1942. *Private collection.*

Similar to the orchestration folios, ten thousand advance artist copies of the six *Wizard of Oz* musical numbers were distributed free to nightclub bands, radio singers, and cafè and hotel entertainers. The deleted "Jitterbug" song was among those issued, the earliest copies of which credited Buddy Ebsen—not Jack Haley—as portraying the Tin Woodman. (Ebsen was forced to resign from the role due to a near-fatal allergic reaction to his metallic makeup. Interestingly, however, his voice remained on the film's soundtrack in choruses for "The Jitterbug" as well as "We're Off to See the Wizard" even after being replaced by Haley.)

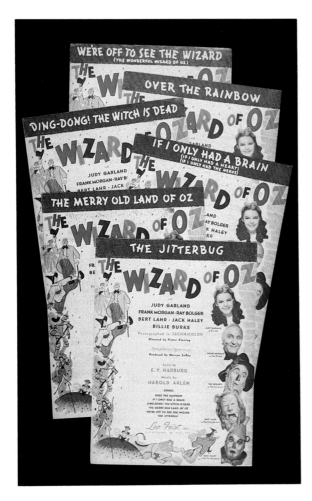

Shortly before national release of MGM's *The Wizard of Oz* in 1939, music publisher Leo Feist, Inc. issued songsheets for six musical numbers featured in the picture. However, once it was decided that "The Jitterbug" song would be excised from the final version of the film, printing of the accompanying sheet music ceased and the song was no longer listed on the covers for later printings of the other selections.

Leo Feist published "Six Song Hits From The Wizard of Oz" in 1939 to test public response to a folio containing all of the film's songs. The cover was identical to the other *Wizard* songsheet art.

Decca presents the Musical Score from METRO-GOLDWYN-MAYER'S Motion Picture Triumph The Wizard of Oz. One of the first film scores ever to be issued, this four-record 78 RPM set originally retailed for $1.69 and was accompanied by a four-page prospectus highlighting the careers of song composers Harold Arlen and E.Y. Harburg. As part of this musical arrangement, Decca included Judy Garland's renditions of "Over the Rainbow" and the suppressed "Jitterbug" song on the album as well as other numbers from the movie as performed by Victor Young and his orchestra with the Ken Darby Singers.

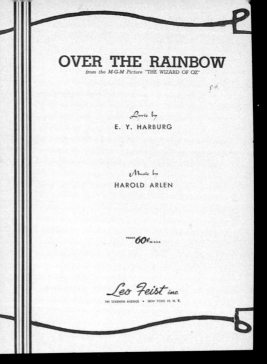

Plans for this *Wizard of Oz Souvenir Album* folio got underway in January, 1940, though the songbook was copyrighted 1939. The layout of the original fifty-cent edition incorporated a great many movie stills combined with Ozzy art work. In later years, the folio was reprinted in less elaborate format and the price printed on the cover increased to $1.00, $1.25, and $1.50.

Leo Feist reprinted the songs made famous in the MGM Oz film in plain white wrappers circa 1945. *Courtesy Michael Gessel.*

Decca Records' *The Musical Score of The Wizard of Oz* was distributed between 1947 and 1948 as part of the Judy Garland Personality Series of recordings. The songs were available as a 78 RPM four-record set (left) or as a 10-inch LP record (right).

British counterparts to each of the six MGM film songsheets (including "The Jitterbug") were published in 1940 by Francis Day & Hunter Ltd. in arrangement with American publisher Leo Feist.

In 1949, MGM Records released
*Songs From the MGM Technicolor
Picture The Wizard of Oz* as a 78
RPM two-record set to further fuel
the success of the recent reissue of
the 1939 film.

Golden Records produced two 78
RPM singles of the *Wizard of Oz*
film's most recognizable songs in
1950. ''Over the Rainbow'' was also
issued in an alternate jacket
depicting Dorothy watching ''birds
fly over the rainbow.''

Prompted by the enthusiastic 1949
re-release of MGM's *The Wizard of
Oz*, Capitol Records issued an
excellent musical adaptation of
Baum's fourth Oz book, *Dorothy
and the Wizard in Oz*, as a three-
record 78 RPM set (left) and as a
boxed set of 45 RPM records (right).
*Boxed set courtesy Chris
Sterling.*

In 1956, MGM Records released
The Wizard of Oz as one of the very
first LP albums to be composed of
actual song and dialogue taken
directly from an original motion
picture soundtrack. Also available
as a small boxed set of 45 RPM
records, the recording was later
offered as a premium through
Proctor & Gamble in 1961, editions
of which were marked as such on
the back of the album jacket. Oddly,
the record label listed ''The Merry
Old Land of Oz''—as would all
future soundtrack labels—even
though the song had been edited
from the recording.

The Hanky Pank Players presented their version of *The Wizard of Oz* as released by Cricket Records in the late 1950s (left). In the 1970s, the same recording was packaged in a newly designed cover under the "Mr. Pickwick Players" label (right). *Courtesy Bill Beem.*

The Wizard of Oz was one of eight deluxe boxed four-record sets produced in 1961 by the Living Literature series. This set contained a facsimile edition of the original book as published the previous year by Dover. *Courtesy Cathi Dentler.*

In addition to its full-length song album, Leo Feist published *The Wizard of Oz Made Simplified* in 1957 with large notes and words for beginning musicians (left). In 1969, the folio featured different cover art and was expanded to include "The Jitterbug," "Lullaby League and Lollypop (sic) Guild," "Optimistic Voices," "Munchkinland," and "If I Were King of the Forest" (right). *Courtesy Rob Roy Macveigh.*

About 1962, MGM Records released *The Wizard of Oz* backed with *Babes in Toyland* as one in a series of ten "Great Children's Stories" (left). Oddly, the cast of the recording followed the dialogue of the MGM motion picture soundtrack verbatim. In 1967, the recording was reissued as a "Leo the Lion" record in a new jacket with artwork clearly patterned after the "Off to See the Wizard" cartoon characters (right). *Courtesy Rob Roy MacVeigh.*

The popularity of the repeated telecasts of *The Wizard of Oz* prompted this double-jacket edition of the MGM soundtrack with new cover art and revised liner notes circa 1962. The album was sold in this format for many years but was eventually reduced to a standard single jacket circa the early 1980s when it was distributed through MCA.

As part of its extensive "Show 'N Tell" line of record and slide-strip packets, General Electric issued *The Wizard of Oz* in 1964.

The *Wizard of Oz* songbook also underwent revision about 1962. The changes included the album jacket cover art and a different, streamlined interior design. A late-1970s edition is shown here, however a slightly more elaborate British version was printed in England in 1973 by the London division of Robbins Music Corporation.

Also in 1964, Peter Pan Records introduced a 78 RPM production of *The Wizard* with its own original songs (top). The same recording was issued in a new jacket shortly afterwards (center) and, by 1971, the audio narrative had become one of Peter Pan's line of book and record sets (bottom).

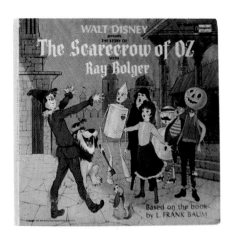

The Wizard of Oz as presented by
the Traveling Playhouse was
released between 1964 and 1965.

In 1965, Disneyland Records
released *Walt Disney Presents the
Story of The Scarecrow of Oz with
Ray Bolger* as a book and record
based on Baum's 1915 story as
narrated by the MGM film
Scarecrow. The record jacket was
issued with two different back
covers: one with an illustration from
the attached storybook and the
other picturing Bolger in his famous
Oz movie role. *Courtesy Bill Beem.*

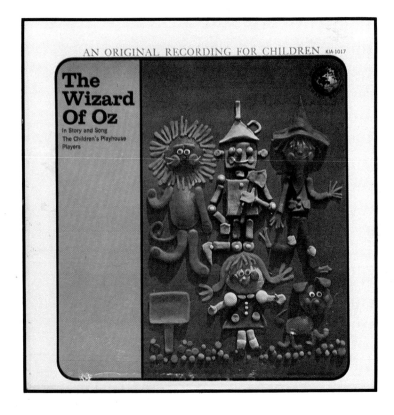

Sears, Roebuck and Company
issued *The Wizard of Oz in Story
and Song* in 1965.

Rocking Horse Records produced
*The Wizard of Oz & Other Favorite
Children's Stories* circa the mid-
1960s. *Courtesy Cathi Dentler.*

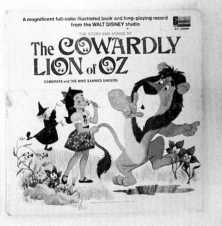

The Children's Playhouse Presents The Wizard of Oz (1969, RCA Camden) featured a children's chorus and a small orchestra singing an arrangement of the familiar MGM motion picture score. *Courtesy* The Baum Bugle.

In 1969, Disneyland Records released two albums which featured songs from the MGM movie. *The Story and Songs of The Wizard of Oz* (left) came replete with a full-color illustrated interior booklet while *The Songs from The Wizard of Oz* (right) featured additional songs "about the Scarecrow and the Cowardly Lion" on its flip side.

An original sequel to the first Oz story, *The Wizard of Oz Returns* was produced by Golden Records in the late 1960s. The album's double jacket opened into a game board and included a separate spinner/playing piece/instruction card combination. The same recording (minus the game) was sold in 1972 as *The Further Adventures of The Wizard of Oz. Courtesy Bill Beem.*

The Story and Songs of The Cowardly Lion of Oz was copyrighted 1968 and released in 1969 as a book and record through the Walt Disney Studio. Though claiming to be based on Ruth Plumly Thompson's book, the narrative was completely original and incorporated a number of songs previously written for Disney's aborted 1950s film musical *The Rainbow Road to Oz. Courtesy Bill Beem.*

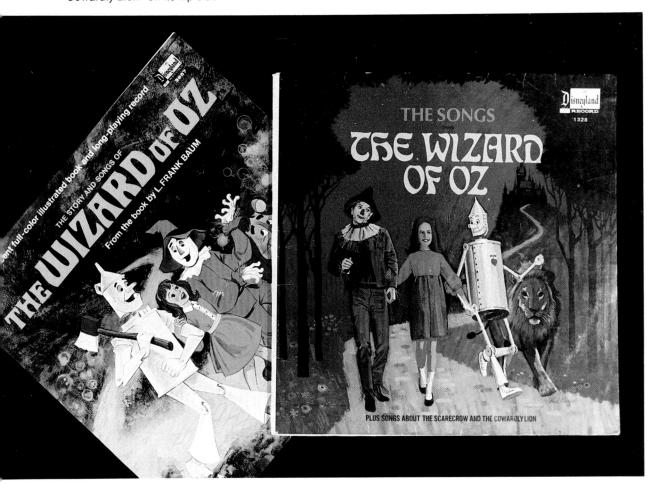

A late-1940s recording of *The Wizard* as narrated by Art Carny was issued in a number of formats throughout the 1950s, 1960s and 1970s as released through Wonderland Records (formerly A.A. Records). Above left is a book and record edition; above right is a 33 1/3 RPM version with additional stories included.

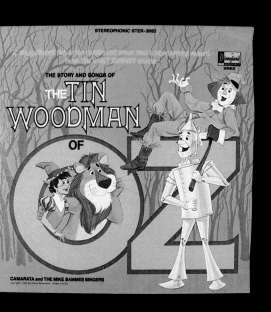

Early editions of this 1969 Disneyland book and record, inspired by 1918's *The Tin Woodman of Oz*, credited Ruth Plumly Thompson—not L. Frank Baum—as author. Later editions corrected the error. *Courtesy Cathi Dentler.*

Never out of print since becoming an immediate best-seller in 1939, the sheet music for "Over the Rainbow" remained a perennial favorite for over fifty years. The most recent version, initially printed in the 1960s, appropriately featured a large portrait of Judy Garland as Dorothy.

The Peter Pan Records' *Wizard of Oz* book and record set was revised with new artwork in the mid-1970s.

A special promotional edition of the *Wizard* soundtrack was available in 1970 exclusively through a Singer Sewing Machine Company offer in conjunction with its sponsorship of the film's twelfth annual television broadcast. The traditional recording was sold at a discount price of $1.50 in a newly-designed jacket that matched a premium poster also distributed by Singer that year.

Hanna-Barbera's popular animated "Snagglepuss" character hosted this *Wizard of Oz* retelling, originally issued in 1965 and re-released in a new jacket (shown here) in 1971. *Courtesy Bill Beem.*

The score of the daily "Magic Moment" presentation at Banner Elk, North Carolina's Land of Oz was made available in the 1970s to the theme park's guests on a 33 1/3 RPM recording which included "Over the Rainbow" from the MGM film in addition to thirteen other original musical numbers.

The Wonderful Wizard of Oz was one of Children's Records of America's ten book and record sets issued in 1974. *Courtesy Cathi Dentler.*

A British edition of the MGM *Wizard of Oz* soundtrack was issued by Robbins Music Corporation circa 1970s in a one-record, double-jacket format. Distributed by Polydor, the record was part of a Silver Screen Soundtrack Series.

The Superscope Story Teller Presents The Wizard of Oz was a small hardcover book packaged with a cassette in 1975. One of thirty such sets, the Oz edition was still available through school supply catalogues into the 1990s as produced by Tele-Story.

The original cast recording of Broadway's *The Wiz* (containing the catchy "Ease On Down the Road") was produced by Atlantic Records in 1975. The following year, the album received a Grammy Award as Best Cast Show Album. *Courtesy Bill Beem.*

In 1976, Caedmon Records commissioned performer (and MGM movie Scarecrow) Ray Bolger to narrate L. Frank Baum's *The Wizard of Oz*. The resulting recording proved a faithful retelling of the famous story interjected with the originality and humor of Bolger's dialogue. Other Oz and related recordings in the series which were read by Bolger and available on record or cassette included *Queen Zixi of Ix* (1979), based on Baum's 1905 fantasy, *The Land of Oz* (1979) and *Little Oz Stories* (1983), based upon episodes from Baum's "Queer Visitors From the Marvelous Land of Oz" comic page. All four recordings were collectively packaged in 1983 as *The Oz Soundbook*.

In 1978, Disney Records issued a reduced-size version of their 1969 *Wizard of Oz* book and record set. Though slightly revised from its previous publication, the new set was also available with audio cassette.

Indicative of the broad appeal of Oz, a "disco" version of the MGM songs and score was released in 1978 by Millenium Record Company and distributed through Casablanca Record and Film Works. Hi-tech musician "Meco" Monardo translated the film's music into a continuous-play, high-energy dance album climaxed by a symphonic overture of many of the movie's themes.

Big Three Publishing printed this sheet music which incorporated "Over the Rainbow" and "We're Off to See the Wizard" as performed by Meco on the accompanying 1978 disco version of the film's orchestration. While composers E.Y. Harburg and Harold Arlen received no credit on the album itself, proper notice of their historic contributions was printed in the songsheet.

In 1978, the Kid Stuff Repertory Company produced *Songs From The Wiz* to coincide with the film's release. Kid Stuff was also responsible for *The Story of The Wizard of Oz* in the late 1970s and *The Land of Oz* (1978). *Courtesy Bill Beem.*

Accomplished composers Sammy Cahn and James Van Heusen originally copyrighted their *Journey Back to Oz* songs in 1962 when the animated motion picture had its beginnings. Eighteen years later, the film's repeated television broadcasts led to this soundtrack album being issued as a Texize product premium in 1980. *Courtesy Bill Beem.*

Pianist Peter Nero released his themes from *The Wiz* in 1977 through Crystal Clear Records. The full-sized album produced in West Germany played at 45 RPM and was backed with several contemporary 1970s pop hits as interpreted by Nero.

The original motion picture soundtrack for *The Wiz* (1978, MCA Records) was a double record album containing an illustrated movie booklet. Featuring the singing voices of stars Diana Ross and Michael Jackson, the record was produced by Quincy Jones, who likewise wrote the film's score. *Courtesy Bill Beem.*

In 1980, the Radiola Company issued this LP recording of the "complete, unedited" Lux Radio Theatre production of *The Wizard of Oz* as it was broadcast on December 25, 1950—once again starring Judy Garland as Dorothy!

Previously issued on the Decca label, *The Musical Score of The Wizard of Oz / The Song Hits from Walt Disney's Pinocchio* was released by MCA Records in 1980 as shown here. Concurrently made available in "picture disc" format, the Oz side of this LP record consisted of the film's songs— including "The Jitterbug"—as performed by Judy Garland and Victor Young and his orchestra for the original 78 RPM Decca record set in 1939.

This circa 1980s audio cassette package from The Mind's Eye promised a "lively, new production" based on L. Frank Baum's original book—even though Bert Lahr's Cowardly Lion on the cover might have indicated otherwise! Total playing time: two hours and eight minutes.

Audio Book Company's circa 1985 *Wizard of Oz* package promised the Baum story in its liner notes but the box drew its unauthorized likenesses from the familiar MGM movie characters.

A *Return to Oz* book and record was released in 1985 by Buena Vista Records. The twenty-four page booklet featured a color movie still on each page while the accompanying 7-inch, 33 1/3 RPM recording provided narration, sound effects and musical background.

On June 29, 1939, NBC devoted its final "Maxwell House Good News" radio broadcast of the season in its entirety to Metro-Goldwyn-Mayer's forthcoming screen version of *The Wizard of Oz*. In addition to Fanny Brice, Hanley Stafford, Meredith Willson, and host Robert Young, the program featured live song and dialogue from Oz celebrities Judy Garland, Ray Bolger, Bert Lahr, Frank Morgan—and even Fred Stone, the Scarecrow from the original 1902 stage play. In 1988, Jass Records released an LP recording of the complete show as originally broadcast (minus a few commercials) which included scripted making-of-the-movie events and Judy Garland's unintentional slip on some "Over the Rainbow" lyrics.

Toys and Novelties

"The Scarecrow of Oz Answers Questions by Radio" was a small cardboard folder distributed to book and department stores by Reilly & Lee in 1924. (Note the shop imprint on the back cover.) The novelty had nothing in common with radio airwaves but did use magnetic force to draw the metal arrow to the correct response when the interior circular dial was set to the desired question. The answer key also referred users to the particular Oz book in which the correct information could be found by providing the number of such title as it appeared in "The Famous Oz Books" listing, conveniently located just inside the folder's front cover. Reilly & Lee always listed *The Land of Oz* as the first Oz book since *The Wizard of Oz* was published by Bobbs-Merrill. *Private collection.*

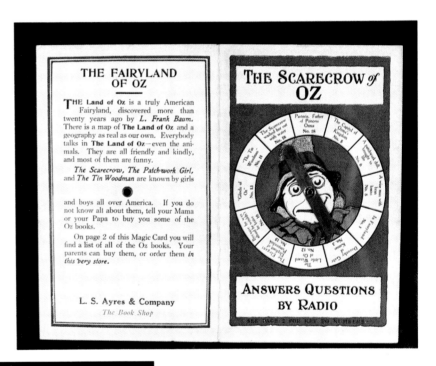

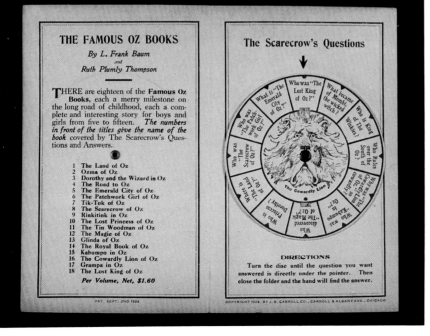

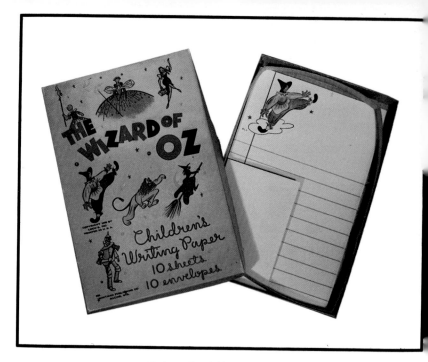

The White and Wychoff Company's Oz stationery featured full-color illustrations patterned after both Denslow and Neill character portrayals. The small note cards were originally packaged as a boxed set in 1925. *Courtesy Michael Gessel.*

Whitman's 1939 boxed set of *Wizard of Oz Children's Writing Paper* contained ten sheets of ruled paper individually illustrated with one of the Al Hirschfeld movie caricatures. (Hirschfeld's Oz artwork was used extensively throughout the film's promotion and could likewise be seen in advertisements, on sheet music and incorporated into movie posters.) Ten minute envelopes were also included.

As one in its line of toy carpet sweepers, Bissell manufactured a child-sized version of its adult *Wizard of Oz* sweeper in 1939 with slight changes to the decal art. *Courtesy Michael Patrick Hearn; photo: Cynthia Dorfman.*

This tin toy watch depicting the MGM Scarecrow and Tin Man was one in a series of famous movie star and cartoon character "timepieces" made in Occupied Japan and sold in the United States circa late-1940s to early-1950s.

This Oz charm bracelet featuring four of the book characters was both undated and unidentified but may have been produced circa the 1950s when children's charm bracelets were in vogue. *Courtesy Michael Patrick Hearn; photo: David Moyer.*

An unidentified manufacturer issued this acrylic Oz paint-by-number circa late-1950s to early-1960s. Interestingly enough, the painting featured not only the standard *Wizard* characters, but also the boy, Tip, and the Sawhorse—both from Baum's *The Land of Oz. Courtesy Cathi Dentler.*

Carefully sculpted character figures and exceptional diorama-like sets made the Sawyer Company's twenty-one scene, three-reel *Wonderful Wizard of Oz* View-Master packet a faithful adaptation of Baum's original narrative. Since its first appearance in 1957 (left; later issue above right), this optical toy set has experienced remarkable longevity, having been issued by Sawyer in True-Vue transparencies and later distributed by GAF (bottom right) in both the traditional and Talking View-Master formats.

Broadway producer John H. Harris directed the 1960-61 Ice Capades which featured a figure skating version of *The Wizard of Oz.* The felt souvenir banner for that presentation was also available in red.

In 1961 the Lowe Company marketed a *Wizard Slate From Oz* "based on the new TV series 'Tales of the Wizard of Oz'." *Courtesy Rob Roy MacVeigh.*

The tan or white envelope packets containing the accessories for each "Showboat" play were also available separately from Remco as replacement parts.

For Christmas 1962, Remco introduced an elaborate pink plastic "Showboat" theater complete with script, die-cut scenery, and characters for four famous stories, *The Wizard of Oz* included.

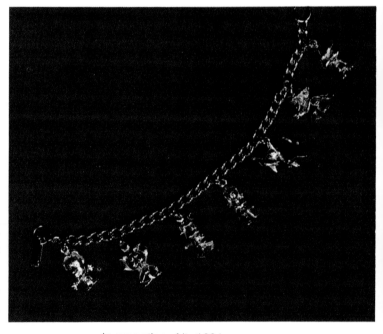

In promotion of its 1964 sponsorship of the *Return to Oz* animated television special, General Electric issued a pot-metal charm bracelet of the movie's characters. The figures from left to right are: The Wizard, Dandy Lion, Rusty the Tin Man, Dorothy, Toto, The Wicked Witch of the West, and Socrates, the Scarecrow.

236

Long a staple of Mardi Gras celebrations, this 1964 token coin featured Bert Lahr's Cowardly Lion and was inscribed "We Return to the Land of Oz."

As sponsors of the *Wizard of Oz* movie telecasts for 1965 and 1969, Proctor & Gamble offered a set of eight plastic hand-puppets free with the purchase of select products. For twenty-five cents and proof-of-purchase, Oz fans could also send away for a cardboard theater, the Wizard puppet and an original adaptation of the story in script form—in which the Wicked Witch of the West repented her evil ways!

A sight and sound combination, Lorob Industries' *Wizard of Oz Action Forms* (1964) was one of twelve such novelties that included a record along with punch-out scenery and character figures which were jointed for movement when properly assembled.

Mattel's "Off to See the Wizard" talking glove puppet originally sold in a decorated box from 1968 to 1970. When the pull-string was drawn, the cartoon characters would randomly repeat up to ten different phrases. Voice-over actress June Foray (best known as the voices of "Rocky the Squirrel" and "Natasha" from the "Bullwinkle" cartoon series) provided Dorothy's dialogue.

When the built-in hand crank was turned, Mattel's "Scarecrow-in-the-Box" sprung from his metal confines to the tune of "Hail! Hail! The Gang's All Here!" The 1967 toy was an "Off to See the Wizard" TV tie-in.

This twenty-piece "Off to See the Wizard" punch-out wall decoration set was printed by Shepard Press Inc. in 1967 for the Homestead Mail Order Company. It was initially made available through a *TV Guide* offer.

An arrangement of "Off to See the Wizard" product premiums from 1967-68. Left: iron-on transfers from Frit-O-Lay; top: Fun Incorporated's *Wizard of Oz Magic Kit* available through Swift Premium Hot Dogs, and sold in magic and novelty shops into the early 1980s; right: two in a series of plastic hand-puppets packaged in boxes of Scooter Pies. *Courtesy Rob Roy MacVeigh.*

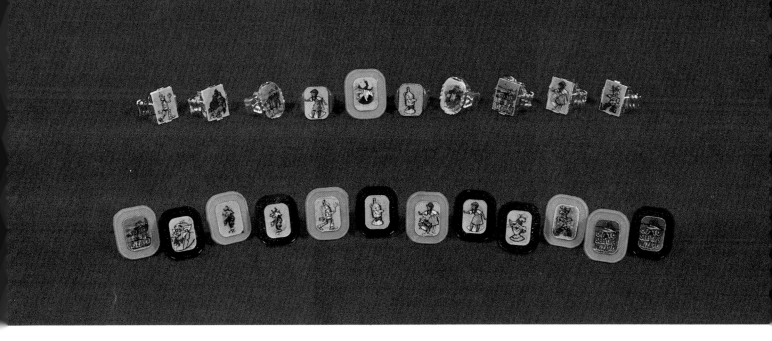

Vari-Vue produced twelve "Off to See the Wizard" "flasher" rings which were dispensed in gumball machines in 1967-68. Picturing the show's six characters on two rings each, the earliest styles were silver-painted resin with a "V" insignia on either side of the finger band. Later varieties were gold-painted, or dark or light blue plastic. *Courtesy Chris Sterling.*

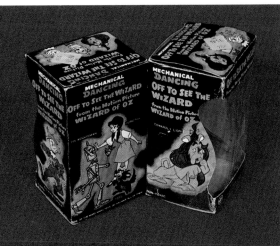

Three plastic *Mechanical Off to See the Wizard Dancing Toys* were marketed in 1967 by Louis Marx & Company. They were available in a boxed set through Montgomery Ward (top) or packaged individually for general retail sale (bottom). When their keys were wound, each toy spun furiously in circles. *Individual boxes courtesy Chris Sterling.*

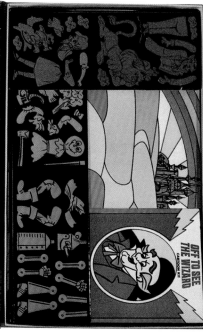

Colorforms' 1967 *Off to See the Wizard Cartoon Kit* included a laminated display board, instruction booklet and thirty-eight colored plastic character pieces.

In 1968, Jiffy Pop Popcorn included sets of *Off to See the Wizard Magic Picture Kits* in its product packaging. Each set contained a sheet of rub-on color transfers and a background picture depicting one of four scenes from the well-known story. They included "Follow the Yellow Brick Road," "Dorothy Melts the Witch," "In the Emerald City" and "The Wizard is Exposed." *Courtesy Chris Sterling.*

For 1968, Kenner added an "Off to See the Wizard" color slide strip to its diverse line of toy projector "Give-A-Show" slides. As late as 1970, the strip sold for $1.19 in a box with four other slides.

In 1968, Craft Master marketed three separate "Off to See the Wizard" boxed paint by number sets. Each set included six paints, a brush and a picture of either the Tin Man, the Scarecrow or the Cowardly Lion. *Courtesy Bob Roy.*

The *Wizard of Oz Stand-Up Rub-Ons* assortment was issued in 1968 by Hasbro. This playset combined the traditional book characters (as inspired by the 1950 Random House abridgement's illustrations) with a unique color transfer concept.

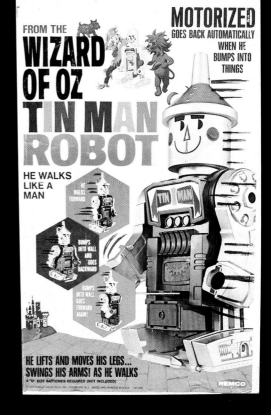

In 1969, Remco Industries produced its battery-operated, motorized 21½-inch tall Tin Man robot "from The Wizard of Oz" as shown on the toy's box label. *Courtesy Rob Roy MacVeigh.*

An oversized 16″ x 18″ *Wizard of Oz* boxed paint-by-number set was sold by Hasbro in 1969. The kit contained eighteen watercolor paint cakes, a brush, two plastic frames and eight pictures to color. *Courtesy Rob Roy MacVeigh.*

Hasbro's 1973 *Wizard of Oz Oil Paint by Number Coloring Set* contained six oil paints, an artist's brush, and one heavy cardboard canvas to be painted.

Although the exact date and origin of these "flasher" disks is unknown, they, along with a Scarecrow disk, were most likely issued in the mid-1970s. Sometime in the 1980s, a company named Global Industries modified the flashers to produce earrings for commercial sale.

Hasbro's *Wizard of Oz* toy and craft line continued in 1973 with a boxed "Stitch-A-Story" set which included two framed fabric pictures, thread, and an embroidery needle.
Courtesy Rob Roy Macveigh.

Ohio Art produced its thirty-piece *The Land of Oz* tea set in the early-to mid-1970s. *Courtesy Dana Ryan.*

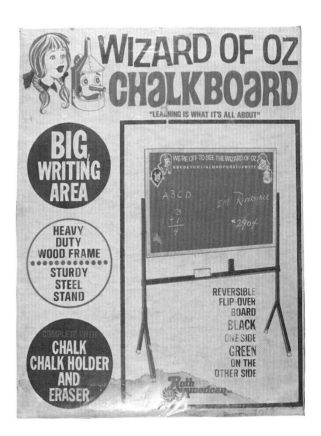

A large *Wizard of Oz* chalkboard was introduced in 1975 by Roth American, a company which also marketed an Oz toy chest the same year.

Cheinco Playthings' movie-based
metal crayon box was licensed by
Metro-Goldwyn-Mayer and sold in
1975.

Friends Industries offered fans of
the MGM movie a large boxed
Wizard of Oz découpage kit in 1975.
The set contained all the materials
necessary to make two wooden
plaques featuring scenes from the
1939 motion picture classic. Also in
1975, the company marketed a
similar kit for making Oz stained
glass ornaments.

Three individual Oz découpage kits
were likewise made available by
Friends Industries in 1975.

This *Wizard of Oz Cast 'n Paint* set
was introduced in 1975 by Friends
Industries. The plaster figures to be
made using the kit materials were
directly modeled after the 1974
Seymour Mann porcelain figurines.
A similar *Wizard of Oz Model Craft*
set using red rubber molds was
advertised as having been
manufactured by the Kay Stanley
Company circa 1950.

Wind-up walking toys of the MGM
Scarecrow, Tin Woodman, and
Cowardly Lion were manufactured
in 1975 by Durham Industries.

This set of three MGM *Wizard of Oz*
inspired water guns was distributed
in 1976 by Durham Industries.
Oddly enough, a slight variant of the
Tin Man toy was reissued—
unauthorized—in 1989 in different
packaging marked "Made in
China."

Durham Industries also offered two
different *MGM's Wizard of Oz "Spin
Around" Wind-Up Ruby Red Slipper*
toys in 1975. Whether a Scarecrow
version was ever marketed is
unknown.

As an educational service to
schools, MovieStrip added a
filmstrip and audio cassette kit of
MGM's *The Wizard* to its product
line in 1976. The package included
two filmstrips and two cassette
tapes in addition to fifteen "activity
cards" with movie scenes designed
to motivate group discussion.

The Ansehl Company of St. Louis was responsible for a great number of Oz toiletry kits including boxed sets of bath beads, talc, lipsticks, perfumes and bubble bath. All of the movie-based products were marked "© 1976 Metro-Goldwyn-Mayer."

A series of plastic figural MGM *Wizard of Oz* Christmas ornaments was introduced by the Bradford Novelty Company for the 1977 holiday season. They measured approximately 4½ inches in height and their appearance was heavily inspired by Mego's popular line of Oz dolls. Similar Munchkin ornaments were available as well.

This *Wizard of Oz* magic slate was issued in 1976 by Whitman/Western Publishing as part of the company's line of Oz activity items.

In 1977, the Bradford Novelty Company also manufactured at least four different sets of *Wizard of Oz Christmas Decorations...With Scenes From the Original MGM Movie Starring Judy Garland*. As a bonus, a cutout picture of the four main characters was printed on the back of each box.

The *Wizard of Oz Magic Story Cloth* made in 1978 by Raco included a small pack of crayons and a sponge so that the covering could be colored, wiped clean, and reused.

In 1979, the Xerox Corporation, in association with *Weekly Reader*, produced a special *Wizard of Oz* storytelling kit teaching guide for elementary age students. The packet contained teacher guidelines, a recorded summary of the story, a mimeograph of the book's secondary characters, and punchouts to assemble a mobile and Emerald City diorama.

One of the very few items merchandised in connection with the 1978 movie *The Wiz* was this three-reel View-Master packet with story booklet issued by GAF.

The Wizard of Oz Fast Dry Acrylic Paint by Number was sold in 1979 by Craft House although the box cover was marked only "© 1939 Loew's Ren. 1966 MGM."

The Scarecrow, Tik-Tok, and Gump from Disney's *Return to Oz* were offered as plush hand-puppets through a send-away promotion sponsored by Welch's Jelly in the summer of 1985.

As part of their 1985 *Return to Oz* promotion, Waldenbooks issued free sheets of movie character stickers to customers who purchased any Oz book title.

Western/Golden's *Return to Oz* magic slate pictured several of the movie's main characters around its borders. *Courtesy Tricia Trozzi.*

Return to Oz children's sunglasses depicting "The Scarecrow" were reportedly sold in the Disney theme parks in summer 1985. These and identically designed blue plastic glasses picturing "Tik-Tok" were also Roy Rogers restaurant premiums. *Courtesy Tricia Trozzi.*

A set of vinyl-and-cloth hand-puppets offered by Presents in 1989 was very similar to the company's own line of concurrently marketed *Wizard of Oz* dolls.

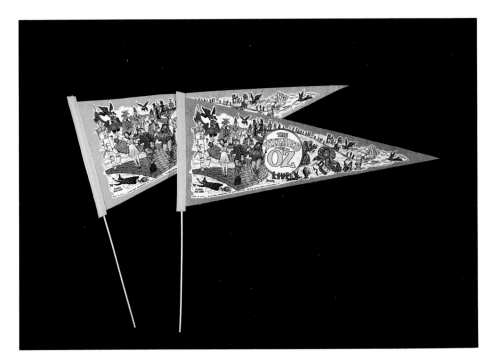

Two souvenir banners featured characters and scenes from the 1989 arena tour production *The Wizard of Oz Live! Courtesy Chris Sterling.*

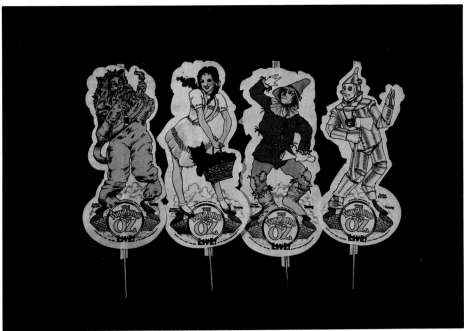

This set of four stick puppets depicted the main characters from *The Wizard of Oz Live!* (1989). *Courtesy Chris Sterling.*

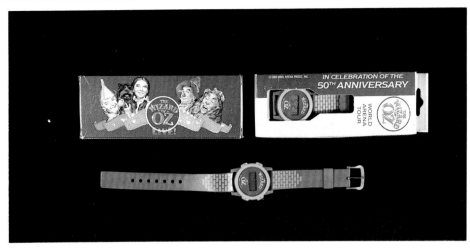

Another inexpensive souvenir of the *Wizard of Oz Live!* arena tour production was this small plastic-and-vinyl LCD wristwatch.

Licensed in 1988 and made available in 1989 was a set of six vinyl-headed *Wizard of Oz* hand-puppets manufactured by the Multi Toys Corporation of Cresskill, New Jersey.

In promotion of its month-long *Wizard of Oz* festivities in 1989, Macy's department stores offered its very own Oz Time watch ("It's Oz Time at Macy's" was the slogan), which was ten dollars with any twenty-five-dollar purchase. Sponsored by the *New York Times*, the Macy's Oz celebration—running from August 13 through September 9—was perhaps the most spectacular of the many ceremonies held across the country in honor of the fiftieth anniversary of the MGM motion picture.

For those Oz fans who somehow managed to *save* some spare change during the onslaught of fiftieth anniversary collectibles made available in 1989, Enesco offered this set of three ceramic character banks.

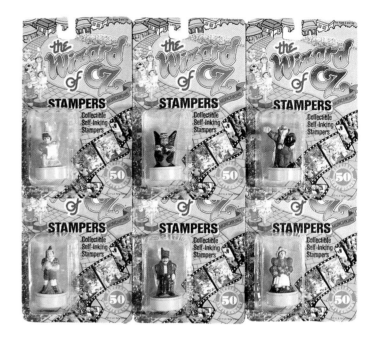

Twelve different figural, self-inking stampers produced by the Multi Toys Corporation in 1989 included the four principal Oz characters, the good and wicked witches, five Munchkins and a winged monkey.

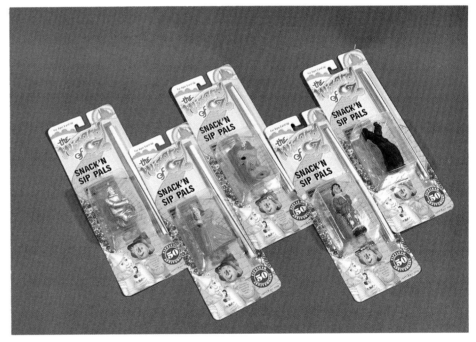

Produced by Multi Toys Corporation in 1989, twelve different *Wizard of Oz Snack 'N Sip Pals* drinking straws provided youngsters with Ozzy enjoyment during snack time and mealtime. (Not shown here is the "Dorothy" straw.)

Multi Toys also marketed Oz vinyl stickers both as individual sets and as part of a playset package (1989).

In 1989, E.K.O. Corporation marketed an Oz quartz wristwatch (similar in most respects to the Oz Time watch offered exclusively by Macy's a few months earlier) as well as a child-size LCD wristwatch. Both were licensed by Turner Entertainment Company.

The Wizard of Oz Umbrella and *Glinda's Magic Wand* were yet two more items manufactured by the Multi Toys Corporation in conjunction with the fiftieth anniversary of the MGM Oz movie. With the aid of two AA batteries, the wand would light up at the touch of a switch.

Included among the various art craft kits produced by Art Award during 1989 were three different *Wizard of Oz Paint by Number Sets* as well as a *Paint With Crayons Kit*, all four of which were licensed by Turner Entertainment Company.

"Wind them up and watch them follow the yellow brick road!" Multi Toys' set of six *Wizard of Oz Wind-Up Walkers* included Glinda, Cowardly Lion, Wicked Witch of the West, Tin Man, Dorothy, and Scarecrow (1989).

Western Publishing issued yet another *Wizard of Oz* magic slate in 1989—this time based upon the 1939 movie classic.

Especially suited to those young ladies favoring the MGM Oz motion picture were several novelty items marketed by Multi Toys Corporation in 1989. These included an Oz storage tin container, a decorated musical jewelry box, and even one-size-fits-all "Ruby Red Slippers." The latter item, of course, was inspired by Judy Garland's famous Oz footwear—which sold for a record $165,000 at a now-legendary Christie's auction in 1988!

Four 12-inch hard plastic *Wizard of Oz* banks were produced by the Multi Toys Corporation (marked "MTC") in 1989. Each sculpted likeness was closely patterned after its movie counterpart. *Courtesy Tod Machin.*

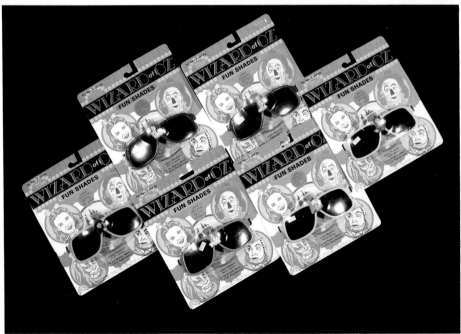

A set of six child-size Ozzy "fun shades" was issued in 1989 by the Multi Kids division of the Multi Toys Corporation.

Wizard of  Collectibles Sources

BEYOND THE RAINBOW. Proprietress Elaine Willingham operates this mail-order business which stocks most contemporary Oz and Judy Garland merchandise including the latest products. For a catalogue, send one dollar and a self-addressed stamped envelope to: Beyond the Rainbow, PO Box 31672, St. Louis, MO 63131, (314) 257-2727. Elaine also offers *Beyond the Rainbow Collector's Exchange*, a bi-monthly Oz newsletter with a classified ad section. A one year subscription of ten dollars may be sent to the above address.

BOOKS OF WONDER deals in contemporary Ozzy merchandise as well as stocking antique and newly reprinted Oz and Baum books. Write or call for catalogue: Books of Wonder, 132 7th Ave. at 18th St., New York, NY 10011, (800) 835-4315.

CAMDEN HOUSE AUCTIONEERS. Since their first auction in 1989, Camden House has consistently listed original *Wizard of Oz* memorabilia in each of its catalogues. To receive notification of their next auction, write or call: Camden House Auctioneers, Inc., 10921 Wilshire Blvd., Suite 713, Los Angeles, CA 90024, (213) 476-1628

FOLLOW THE YELLOW BRICK ROAD DOLL & TOY MUSEUM. This "Mom and Pop" establishment offers a free museum, life-sized replicas of Oz personalities and character toys and collectibles of all kinds for sale. Write or call: Dorothy (who else!) c/o Follow the Yellow Brick Road Doll & Toy Museum, 34 S. Main St., Mullica Hill, NJ 08062, (609) 478-6137.

GRYPHON BOOKSHOP stocks a comprehensive inventory of rare and out-of-print children's books including the Oz book series. Write or call: Gryphon Bookshop, 2246 Broadway (80-81st Sts.), New York, NY 10024, (212) 362-0706.

HAKE'S AMERICANA & COLLECTIBLES. Ted Hake has specialized in character and personality collectibles along with artifacts of popular culture for over twenty-five years. To receive a catalogue of their next three thousand item mail/phone bid auction, send five dollars to: Hake's Americana & Collectibles, PO Box 1444, York, PA 17405.

THE INTERNATIONAL WIZARD OF OZ CLUB. Since 1957, the "Oz Club" has upheld and sustained interest in Oz books, Oz authors and Oz miscellania. The Club publishes a "Journal of Oz," *The Baum Bugle*, three times annually. Collector services which the Club has to offer include *The Oz Trading Post* bulletin whereby members can buy, sell and swap Oz collectibles. A number of regional conventions and gatherings are held each year during which Oz books and related ephemera are auctioned and sold. The conventions also provide a wonderful opportunity to "confer, converse and otherwise hob-nob" with fellow Oz enthusiasts. Annual membership dues of ten dollars may be sent to: Fred M. Meyer, Secretary, 220 N. 11th St., Escanaba, MI 49829.

CORDELIA AND THOMAS PLATT— AUTOGRAPHS AND HISTORICAL MATERIAL. The Platts have specialized in autographs of celebrity, sports and historical personalities for twenty years. They usually have signatures from the MGM *Wizard of Oz* cast in stock. Write or call: Cordelia and Thomas Platt, 1598 Millstone River Road, Belle Mead, NJ 08502, (908) 359-7959

THAT'S ENTERTAINMENT!. Norm Lazarson and Audrea Cohen offer a wide range of Hollywood personality and character collectibles including *The Wizard of Oz*. Write or call: That's Entertainment!, 222 Blue Hills Road, North Haven, CT 06473, (203) 872-9207.

THE YELLOW BRICK ROAD. Manager Jean Nelson and staff maintain a *Wizard of Oz* museum in addition to offering an infinite array of Oz collectibles for sale. Jean is also responsible for organizing Chesterton, Indiana's annual "Wizard of Oz Days" parade and festivities. Write or call: The Yellow Brick Road, 762 S. Calumet, Chesterton, IN 46304, (219) 926-7048.

Bibliography

The following books and select periodicals contain references to *Wizard of Oz* collectibles and/or provide further insight into the manufacture and marketing of similar character merchandise and memorabilia. Several of the titles listed also furnish additional background on the life and written works of L. Frank Baum and other Oz authors:

Axe, John, *The Encyclopedia of Celebrity Dolls* (Maryland: Hobby House Press, 1983)

Burdick, Loraine, *Child Star Dolls and Toys* (Puyallup, Washington: Quest-Eridon Books, 1968; revised 1977)

Chaneles, Sol, *Collecting Movie Memorabilia* (New York: Arco Publishing, 1977)

De Thuin, Richard, *The Official Identification and Price Guide to Movie Memorabilia* (New York: House of Collectibles, 1990)

Eyles, Allen, *The World of Oz* (Tucson, Arizona: HP Books, Inc., 1985)

Greene, David L. and Martin, Dick, *The Oz Scrapbook* (New York: Random House, 1977)

Hanff, Peter, Greene, Douglas G., Martin, Dick, Haff, James E. and Greene, David L., *Bibliographia Oziana* (The International Wizard of Oz Club, Inc., 1976; revised 1988)

Harmetz, Aljean, *The Making of The Wizard of Oz* (New York: Alfred A. Knopf, 1977)

Hearn, Michael Patrick, *The Annotated Wizard of Oz* (New York: Clarkson N. Potter, 1973)

Hegenberger, John, *A Collector's Guide to Treasures From the Silver Screen* (Radnor, Pa: Wallace-Homestead, 1991)

Heide, Robert and Gillman, John, *Starstruck, The Wonderful World of Movie Memorabilia* (New York: Doubleday-Dolphin, 1986)

Judd, Polly, *Cloth Dolls of the 1920s and 1930s* (Maryland: Hobby House Press, 1990)

Longest, David, *Character Toys and Collectibles, Second Series* (Kentucky: Collector Books, 1987)

Markoski, Carol and Gene, *Tomart's Price Guide to Character & Promotional Glasses* (Ohio: Tomart Publications, 1990)

Schiller, Justin, *The Justin G. Schiller Collection of L. Frank Baum and Related Oziana*, auction catalogue (New York: Swann Galleries, Inc., 1978)

Thomas, Rhys, *The Ruby Slippers of Oz* (Los Angeles, Ca: Tale Weaver Publishing, 1989)

Weiss, Hilary, *The American Bandana* (San Francisco, Ca: Chronicle Books, 1990)

Zillner, Dian, *Hollywood Collectibles* (West Chester, Pa: Schiffer Publishing, Ltd., 1990)

MAGAZINES

Antique Toy World, Chicago, Illinois

The Baum Bugle, The International Wizard of Oz Club, Inc.

Collectibles Illustrated, Dublin, N.H. (No longer in publication)

Collector's Showcase, Tulsa, Oklahoma

Doll Reader, Cumberland, Maryland

The Inside Collector, Elmont, New York

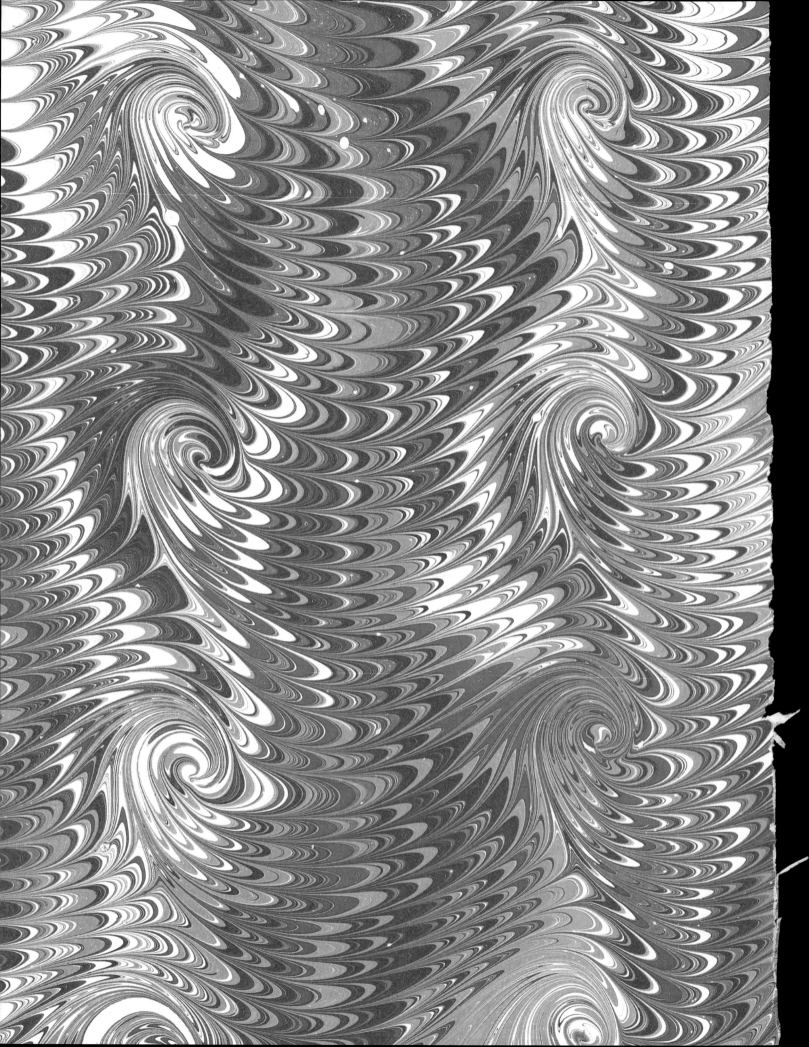

VALUE GUIDE

The following item values are estimates and are intended solely for reference purposes. For each range scale, the lower end estimate generally denotes greater item wear than the upper range estimation. A wider range approximation indicates that a given item is typically found in diverse states of condition. As this book is not all-inclusive, variants for any item illustrated potentially exist. For any collectible not pictured and described in this book, there will hopefully be a similar item catalogued which may be of use in determining value. Independent of this guide's suggested assessments, prices for Oz memorabilia may vary greatly depending upon item condition, rarity, desirability and geographic locale. As these factors may create a vastly fluctuating market, neither the authors nor the publisher assume any responsibility for transaction losses incurred in consultation with this guide.

Position codes are: T=top, TL=top left, TC=top center, TR=top right, CL=center left, C=center, CR=center right, B=bottom, BL=bottom left, BC=bottom center, BR=bottom right, L=left, R=right

Pg	Position	Price Range
39	L	200-400
39	R	800-1,500
40	TL	175-300
40	TR	75-150
40	BL	25-50
41	Top	800-1,000
41	BL	200-400
41	BR	600-900
42	TL	1,000-2,000
42	TR	75-175
42	BR	150-250
43	TR	100-200
43	BL	25-75
43	BR	150-250
44	TL	125-200
44	CR	35-75
44	BL	35-75
45	TL	150-300
45	TR	125-200
45	BL	150-200
45	BR	150-200
46	TR	75-150
46	BL	200-400
46	CR	25-75
47	TL	200-400
47	TR	20-40
47	BL	100-200
47	BR	50-75
48	T	200-300
48	BL	5-15
48	BR	10-20
49	L	175-275
49	R w/dust jacket	200-400
	w/o dust jacket	50-150
49	C	75-275
50	TL each	15-35
50	TR w/o waddles	35-75
51	TL	50-150
51	TR each	15-30
51	BL w/dust jacket	75-150
	w/o dust jacket	15-35
51	BR	20-50
52	TL	20-50
52	BL w/dust jacket	30-50
	w/o dust jacket	10-30
52	T,C each book	10-30
52	BR boxed set	200-400
53	TL	
	w/dust jacket	250-500
	w/o dust jacket	200-400
53	TR	125-250
53	BL	125-250
53	BR	150-275
54	TL w/dust jacket	30-50
	w/o dust jacket	20-40
54	CL w/dust jacket	20-40
	w/o dust jacket	10-20
54	TR	15-30
54	BR each	5-15
55	TL	5-15
55	B each	2-10
55	TR	15-30
55	C	5-15
56	TL	10-25
56	BL	10-25
56	TR	10-20
56	BR	25-50
57	T each	5-15
57	CL	5-20
57	CR	10-25
57	B	10-25
58	TL	5-15
58	TC	10-20
58	TR	5-10
58	BL	10-20
58	BR	10-25
59	TL	15-35
59	TR each	5-15
59	BL	25-75
59	BR	5-10
60	TL each	5-15
60	TR	2-5
60	BL	15-30
60	BR	5-10
61	TL	2-5
61	TR	5-10
61	CL each	10-25
61	BR each	2-10
62	TL each	5-10
62	TR	15-30
62	BL each	10-25
62	BR	20-40
63	TL	15-25
63	C	15-25
63	TR	5-10
63	CL	10-20
63	BR each	5-10
64	TL	15-30
64	TR	10-15
64	BL each	5-15
64	BR each book	2-5
	book display	25-45
65	TL	2-5
65	TR	2-5
65	BL	5-10
65	CR each	2-5
66	TL each	2-5
66	TR each	2-10
66	BL	5-10
66	BR each	5-15
67	TL each	10-20
67	TR	5-10
67	BL	2-5
67	BR	2-5
68	T	5-10
68	B	10-15
69	T each	15-35
69	B	100-200
70	TL	75-150
70	TR,BR each	40-75
70	CR	50-100
70	BL	75-150
71	TL	50-75
71	TR each	5-10
71	BL each	100-200
71	BR each	5-10
72	TL each	5-10
72	TR each	2-5
72	CL	5-10
72	BR	15-25
73	TL each	15-25
73	TR	20-30
73	B each	25-50
74	T each	15-25
74	BL	10-15
74	BR	10-15
75	L	25-75
75	R	20-40
76	TL	.40-75
76	TR	30-50
76	CL	30-50
76	CR	30-50
76	BL	30-50
76	BR	30-50
77	TL	30-50
77	TR each set	20-35
77	CL	40-60
77	BR each	35-50
78	TL,TR,BL, BR each	30-45
79	TL,TR,BL, BR each	30-45
80	TL each set	75-125
80	TR each	20-25
80	BL each	
	music box	50-75
	trinket box	10-25
80	BR each	125-150
81	T set	15-25
81	CL,BL	
	silver set	400-600
	gold set	1,600-1,800
81	CR	40-75
82	TL each	10-25
82	TR	40-60
82	CR each	15-25
82	BL each	25-40
83	TL,TR,BL, BR each	30-45
84	TL,TR,BL, BR each	30-45
85	TL each pair	20-35
85	TR gold finish	35-50
	pewter finish	15-35
85	BL	300-400
86	TL each	10-20
86	TR each	10-20
86	BL	40-60
87	TL each	15-30
87	TR each stamp	1-2
87	BL	350-400
88	TR,CL,BR each	160
89	TL each	25-50
89	R each	15-30
90	TL	15-30
90	TR	15-30
90	BL	15-30
90	BR	15-30
91	TL	15-30
91	TR	5-15
91	BL	15-30
91	BR	15-30
92	TL	5-10
92	TR each	5-15
92	BL each	50-75
92	BR each	40-60
93	TL,TR,BL,BR, ea.	10-20
94	TL,TR, CL,CR each	20-50
94	BR	5-10
95	CL,C,CR each	50-150
96	TL each	700-1,000
96	TC	700-1,000
96	TR	40-75
96	BC	400-800
96	BR each	40-75
97	TL each	10-20
97	BL talking	40-75
	mute	10-30
97	TR,CR,BR each	25-50
98	TL	75-150
98	TC,TR each	50-100
98	B	125-200
99	TL	150-250
99	TR	15-25
99	BL each	50-75
99	BR each	10-20
100	TL	5-15
100	TR	10-20
100	B each	700-1,000
101	T each	20-35
101	C each	20-35
101	B each	25-45
102	T	700-1,000
102	BL	60-80
102	BR	35-50
103	TL,TC,BL each	35-50
103	BR	5-15
104	CL doll	135
	display	195
104	TC	195
104	TR	195
104	BC	195
104	BR	245
105	TL	245
105	TR	
	stuffed dolls each	15-35
	vinyl figures each	5-10
105	CL	195
105	BR each doll	5-15
106	T,C,B each	5-15
107	TL each	15-25
107	TR each	10-25
107	B each	5-15
108		40-60
109	TL	75-275
109	TR,B each	50-100
110	each scarf	100-250
111	TL	50-75
111	TR each	25-45
111	BL	75-125
111	BR	15-25
112	TL	15-30
112	TR	5-15
112	CL each	15-30
112	CR	25-50
112	B	15-25
113	TL each	5-15
113	TR	30-50
113	BL each	5-15
113	BR roll	25-50
114	TL	20-40
114	TR	10-25
114	BL	15-30
114	BR	10-25
115	TL	15-30
115	TR	10-20
115	BL	10-20
115	BR	15-25
116	TL	15-30
116	TR each	5-15
116	CL each	5-10
116	CR set	10-20
116	BL each	15-30
117	TL set	15-30
117	TR	10-25
117	BL	10-20
117	BR each	5-15
118	TL	50-75
118	TR each stamp	5-15
	stamp set	15-25
	display	40-60
118	BL each	10-25
118	BR	15-30
119	TL	10-25
119	TR each box	5-15
	dispenser	5-15
119	BL	25-40
119	BR each	5-10
120	TL,TR,CL, CR,B each	3-10
121	TR	10-20
121	C,CR each	25-40
121	B set	25-50
122	TL each	5-10
122	TR	40-60
122	B each	5-10
123	TL boxed set	125-250
123	TR each	50-150
123	B each	50-125
124	TL each set	50-100
124	TR each	20-40
124	BL each	20-40
124	BR each	30-50
125	TL each	25-50
125	TR	25-50
125	BL each	15-25
125	BR each	30-60
126	TL each	15-30
126	TR each	20-40
126	BL each	400-600
126	BR each	30-50
127	each figurine	75-100
	dome display	50-75
128	TL	40-60
128	TR each	5-15
128	BL each	50-75
128	BR each	35
129	T each	3-10
129	C each	30-50
129	BL each	3-10
129	BR each figure	2-5
	boxed set	15-30
130	TL each	5-10
130	TR set	40-60
130	BL each	40-80
130	BR	145
131		400-800
132	game, version w/figures	400-800
	version w/o figures	150-300

Item	Price
133 book/puzzle sets, each	250-500
134 TL	125-250
134 TR	150-300
134 BL,CR each set	75-150
135 T	25-55
135 C each	20-35
135 B	20-40
136 TL	15-25
136 TR	2-10
136 BL	20-50
136 BR each	15-30
137 TL	2-10
137 TR	2-5
137 B each	5-10
138 TL each	15-30
138 TR	10-20
138 BL	5-10
138 BR	5-10
139 T each	2-5
139 BL	5-15
139 BR	5-15
140 T each	2-10
140 B each	2-10
141 T each	25-75
141 BL	15-30
141 BR each	15-25
142 TL,CL each glass	5-15
142 TR	5-10
142 CR	10-20
142 BR each glass	10-20
143 TL	10-20
143 TR each	5-15
143 CL each	10-25
143 CR	20-35
143 BR each	25-50
144 TL	5-15
144 TR each	10-20
144 CL	10-20
144 CR	5-15
144 BR each	10-20
145 L	15-30
145 R	15-30
146	25-75
147	25-75
148	25-75
149 set of cards	150-300
150 TL	15-25
150 TR	15-25
150 B each	20-40
151 TL	35-65
151 CR	25-50
151 BL	10-20
152 TL each	5-15
152 TR	15-25
152 BR	10-20
153 TL	25-40
153 CR	50-150
153 BL	50-150
154 L	50-150
154 R	50-150
155 TL	50-150
155 CR	5-15
155 B each	2-10
156 TL each	10-20
156 TR	50-150
156 C,BR	20-40
157 TL	15-30
157 TR	15-30
157 BR	25-40
158 TL	5-15
158 CR magazine	50-100
158 BL	5-15
159 L	50-100
159 R	100-200
160 TL	15-30
160 TR	15-30
160 BL	15-30
160 BR	15-30
161 TL each	5-15
161 TR	50-75
161 CR	10-25
161 BL	75-100
162 T	15-30
162 BL	2-5
162 BR	5-10
163 each postcard	25-75
164 T	30-80
164 BL	30-80
164 BR each postcard	30-80
165 TL	25-75
165 CR	10-20
165 B	20-40
166 TR	20-40
166 BL	10-20
166 BR	40-80
167 L	35-75
167 TR each	20-50
167 BL	25-50
167 CR each Oz card	25-50
J. Garland card	5-15
168-169 postcards, each	2-5
170 T each	2-10
170 BL	2-10
170 BR	2-10
171 TL,TR set	15-30
171 B set	20-40
172 T each	2-5
172 BL boxed set	5-15
172 BR boxed set	5-15
173 T each	2-5
173 B boxed set	15-25
174 TL each	2-5
174 TR each	2-5
174 BL	2-5
174 BR	2-5
175 L	60-125
175 R	10,000-15,000
176-177 title card	3,500-5,000
each scene card	1,000-3,000
178 T,B each	9,000-12,000
179 TL	1,500-3,000
179 TR	3,000-5,000
179 BL each	75-125
180 T	200-400
180 CR	750-1,000
180 B	100-200
181 T,B each	500-800
182-183 title card	200-400
each scene card	150-300
184 TL	300-500
184 TR	200-400
184 BL	400-800
184 BR	250-400
185 T	300-500
185 BL	300-500
185 BR	150-300
186-187 title card	100-300
each scene card	75-125
188 CL	300-500
188 TR	5-15
188 BR	20-40
189 TL	30-50
189 TR	5-15
189 BL	30-50
189 BR	10-25
190 TL	5-15
190 TR	5-15
190 BL	5-15
190 BR	40-60
191 TL	40-60
191 TR	10-25
191 BL	50-75
191 BR	5-15
192 TL	5-15
192 TR	5-15
192 BL	15-25
192 BR	15-25
193 TL	15-25
193 CR	5-15
193 CL,B	15-25
194 TL	10-25
194 TR	5-15
194 BL	30-50
194 BR	15-25
195 TL	25-40
195 TR	15-30
195 BL	5-15
195 BR	35-50
196 TL	5-15
196 TR	15-25
196 BL	20-40
196 BR	5-15
197 L	25-50
197 R	20-40
198 TL each	20-50
198 TR	50-100
198 B	75-150
199 complete pressbook	3,000-6,000
200 TL	125-250
200 TR	500-1,000
200 BL,BR	150-300
201 TL each	15-25
201 TR	20-40
201 BL	20-40
201 BR	75-100
202 TL,CL	50-75
202 TR	75-125
202 B	30-60
203 T	20-40
203 CL	60-100
203 CR	25-45
203 B each	15-25
204 TL	50-75
204 CR	5-15
204 B each	15-25
205 TL	5-15
205 TR	5-15
205 BL	15-30
205 BR	5-15
206 TL,TR	15-25
206 BR	15-25
207 T	15-25
207 C	20-35
207 B	15-25
208 T each	5-10
208 CL	10-20
208 CR,B each	25-50
209 TL,TR	25-50
209 B each	10-20
210 T	25-50
210 C	75-150
210 B each	25-50
211 T	5-15
211 C	5-15
211 B each kit	5-10
212 TL	3-10
212 TR	3-10
212 BL display	10-20
clock	15-30
212 BR	10-20
213 L	20-40
213 R	10-20
214 CL	30-60
214 TR	20-50
214 B	20-40
215 TL	30-60
215 TR	50-100
215 BL	35-65
216 TL	20-50
216 TR	30-60
216 BL	35-65
217 TL	15-30
217 TR	15-30
217 B	15-30
218 TL	10-25
218 TR each	20-40
218 BL each	10-20
218 BR	20-35
219 TL "The Jitterbug"	50-100
other titles, each	15-35
219 TR	40-60
219 B	50-125
220 TL original edition	50-100
each reissue	25-50
220 TR	10-20
220 BL each	25-45
220 CR each	40-65
221 TL	25-50
221 TR each	10-20
221 BL each	25-50
221 BR	25-50
222 TL each	5-15
222 TR	30-60
222 C each	15-30
222 B each	5-15
223 TL	10-20
223 TR	5-15
223 BL	5-15
223 BR each	5-15
224 TL	5-15
224 TR	10-25
224 BL	5-15
224 BR	5-15
225 TL	5-15
225 TC	5-20
225 TR	10-25
225 B each	5-10
226 TL,TR each	5-15
226 BL	10-25
226 BR	5-10
227 TL	15-30
227 TR	2-10
227 BL	5-15
227 BR	10-20
228 TL	5-15
228 TR	15-30
228 BL	2-10
228 BR	5-15
229 TL each	5-15
229 TR	10-25
229 BL	2-10
229 BR	5-15
230 T	5-15
230 C	10-25
230 B	5-15
231 T	5-20
231 BL	10-20
231 BR	10-20
232 TL	5-15
232 TR	5-15
232 CR	10-15
232 BL	5-15
233 T,B	50-125
234 TL each sheet	20-40
234 TR	125-250
234 BL	75-275
234 BR	15-30
235 TL	20-40
235 TR	10-25
235 CL original issue	15-25
each reissue	5-15
235 BR	5-20
236 TL	15-30
236 TR	10-20
236 BL	35-75
236 BR	20-40
237 TL	10-25
237 TR each puppet	5-15
theater	30-60
237 CL	15-30
237 BR talking	40-75
mute	10-30
238 CL iron-on	10-25
magic kit	5-20
each puppet	5-20
238 TR	15-35
238 BR	25-50
239 T each	5-15
239 CL,BL each toy	15-40
239 CR	30-50
240 T each	10-20
240 BL	20-50
240 BR	10-20
241 TL	20-40
241 TR	50-125
241 BL	20-40
241 BR	10-20
242 TL	20-40
242 TR each	5-15
242 BL	30-60
242 BR	25-50
243 TL	5-15
243 TR	15-35
243 C	20-40
243 BR each	10-25
244 TL each	20-40
244 TR each	20-40
244 BL each	20-40
244 BR	20-50
245 TL each	15-30
245 TR each	5-15
245 BL	5-15
245 BR each set	20-40
246 T	5-15
246 C	5-15
246 B	10-20
247 T	15-30
247 B each	10-25
248 TL	2-5
248 TR	5-15
248 BL each	5-15
248 BR each	10-20
249 T each	5-15
249 C each	10-20
249 B	5-15
250 TL,TR,CL each	10-20
250 CR	25-50
250 BL each	10-20
251 TL,TR each	5-10
251 CR,B each	5-10
252 T each	5-10
252 CL	15-30
252 BL	5-15
252 CR each	5-10
253 T each	5-15
253 BL each	5-10
253 BR	5-10
254 T each	5-15
254 C each	15-30
254 B each	5-10